how2become

A 999 Fire Control Operator

Richard McMunn

Orders: Please contact How2become Ltd, Suite 3, 50 Churchill Square Business Centre, Kings Hill, Kent ME19 4YU. You can also order via the e mail address info@how2become.co.uk.

ISBN: 978-1910202999. First published 2014

Printed in Great Britain for How2become Ltd by CMP.

CONTENTS

INTRODUCTION

Welcome to 'How 2 Become a 999 Fire Control Operator'. This guide has been designed to help you prepare for and pass the selection process that forms part of the UK Fire Control Operator selection process.

The author of this guide, Richard McMunn, spent over 16 years in the UK Fire Service. He worked at many different fire stations at every position up to Station Manager, and he has also sat on numerous interview panels assessing potential candidates. You will find his advice invaluable and inspiring in your pursuit to joining what is probably one of the most exciting careers available. Whilst the selection process to join the Fire Service as a Control Operator (FCOp) is highly competitive, there are a number of things you can do in order to improve your chances of success, and they are all contained within this guide.

The guide itself has been split up into useful sections to make it easier for you to prepare for each stage. Read each section carefully and take notes as you progress. Don't ever give up on your dreams; if you really want to become a Fire Control

Operator then you can do it. The way to prepare for a job in the Fire Service is to embark on a programme of 'in depth' preparation, and this guide will show you exactly how to do that.

If you need any help with tests or interview help and advice, then we offer a wide range of products to assist you. These are all available through our online shop **www.how2become. com.**

Once again, thank you for your custom and we wish you every success in your pursuit to become a Fire Control Operator. Work hard, stay focused and be what you want...

Best wishes,

The how2become team

The How2become Team

PREFACE BY AUTHOR RICHARD MCMUNN

I joined the Fire Service on January the 25th 1993 as an operational firefighter after completing four years in the Fleet Air Arm branch of the Royal Navy. In the build-up to joining the Fire Service I embarked on a comprehensive training programme that would see me pass the selection process with relative ease. The reason why I passed the selection process with ease was solely due to the preparation and hard work that I had put in during the build-up.

I have always been a great believer in preparation. Preparation was my key to success, and it is also yours. Without the right level of preparation you will be setting out on the route to failure. The Fire Service is very hard to join, but if you follow the steps that I have compiled within this guide then you will increase your chances of success dramatically.

Remember, you are learning how to be a successful candidate, not a successful Fire Control Operator! I also want to state from the offset that, although I spent my career working as

an operational Fire Officer, I have vast experience of how the Fire Service recruits its staff, including Fire Control Operators. I also want to stress that how you prepare for the application and selection process is absolutely pivotal. The Fire Service will assess you predominantly against the **key qualities and attributes** required to perform the role, and these will feature heavily throughout the duration of the content. During your preparation, you do not need to concentrate your efforts on learning any of the operational procedures that are required to be a Fire Control Operator; these will come later, once you start your training.

The Fire Service has changed a great deal over the past few years and even more so in how it assesses potential candidates for firefighters and Fire Control Operator positions. When I joined in 1993, it helped if you were 6ft tall, built like a mountain and from a military background. Things have certainly changed since then, and rightly so. Yes, the Fire Service still needs people of that calibre but it also needs people who represent the community in which it serves. It needs people from different backgrounds, different cultures, different ages, different sexual orientations and different genders.

The men and women of the UK Fire Service carry out an amazing job. They are there to protect the community in which they serve and they do that job with great pride, passion and very high levels of professionalism and commitment. They are to be congratulated for the service they provide.

Before you apply to join the Fire Service, you need to be fully confident that you too are capable of providing that same level of service. If you think you can do it, and you can rise to the challenge, then you just might be the type of person the Fire Service is looking for.

As you progress through this guide you will notice that the qualities required to be a Fire Control Operator are a common theme. You must learn these qualities, and also be able to demonstrate throughout the selection process that you can meet them, if you are to have any chance of successfully passing the selection process.

Best wishes,

Richard McMunn

Richard McMunn

CHAPTER ONE

WHAT IS A FIRE CONTROL OPERATOR?

Thousands of calls are received by the Fire Service control every year, and the Fire Control Operators (FCOp) are a vital element in the work of the Fire and Rescue Service.

The main duty of the FCOp is to obtain enough information from the caller and, within 90 seconds of taking the call, decide what fire crews and equipment need to be sent to the incident. Naturally, in the vast majority of cases this will be a relatively simple task based on the predetermined response that has been set by the Fire and Rescue Service. However, on occasions there will be times when the skills of the FCOp will be tested to the limit. The potential for varying degrees of incident difficulty will very much depend on the 'risks' that are present in a specific county area. For example, as a Fire Officer I served with Kent Fire and Rescue Service and the

 how2become

county of Kent has many diverse and different risks. To name just a few, in Kent there are the following significant risks:

- The Channel Tunnel

- The M2, M20, M25 and M26 motorways

- Dungeness Power Station

- Numerous rail links, including the hi-speed rail link to London

- Bluewater shopping centre

- The Queen Elizabeth Bridge and the Dartford river crossing

Of course, the county area that you are applying to join as a FCOp will have many different risks than the county of Kent. The reason why I am making reference to a county's risks is because I recommend you learn what they are before you attend the interview stage of the FCOp selection process. Here is a sample interview question for you to prepare for:

Q. What are the major risks presented to the Fire and Rescue Service in this county area?

Throughout this book I will give you little tips like this for you to gather and prepare for.

TIP

Learn the major risks within your county area before you attend the interview. You may get asked what they are and why they are a risk to the general public.

In addition to gathering information from a caller it is the responsibility of the FCOp to calm and influence the distressed

caller. This can be a very difficult thing to do, especially if the caller has just been involved in, or witnessed, a highly distressing incident. It is times like this that your skills will be tested to the limit. One of your main tasks is to pinpoint exactly the location of the caller. This can be even harder if the caller is on a motorway or in a rural area. At times, the survival advice you will give members of the public, as a Fire Control Operator over the phone, really will save lives.

Once firefighters have arrived at the incident, the Fire Control Operator will remain in constant contact with the control room to report on the progress of the incident and to request any additional crews or equipment that may be required. They are also a central communication point between firefighters and agencies such as the Police and Ambulance services.

To be a competent FCOp you will need to demonstrate the following personal attributes:

- Confident communication skills (oral, written and comprehension skills);
- Effective and confident telephone communicator;
- Good keyboard skills;
- Be able to work calmly under pressure maintaining attention to detail;
- Enjoy contributing to a small team environment;
- Be able to prioritise events and take appropriate action;
- Be able to absorb verbal and written information and apply this both practically and theoretically to NVQ Level 3 standard or equivalent;
- Be self-motivated, with aptitude and ability to undertake intensive initial and ongoing training and assessment.

I mentioned earlier how important the personal qualities and attributes are to your success. Therefore, one of the very first jobs you have during your preparation is to obtain a copy of the job description and the person specification for the role. These two documents will be the difference between success and failure, simply because they determine how you will be assessed throughout the selection process.

> **TIP**
>
> Obtain a copy of the job description and person specification for the role of a Fire Control Operator. These two documents should be provided within the recruitment pack, or alternatively they can usually be found on the website of the Fire and Rescue Service you are applying to join.

Of course, I will take the time to discuss these two documents at a later point within the guide and how you can use them to improve your chances of success.

When a Fire Control Operator vacancy arises, and after completing the application form, those applicants who are short-listed will be asked to take part in a selection of general ability tests. These tests focus on:

- Listening skills
- English comprehension
- Keyboard accuracy and speed.

Success in these tests leads to a formal interview and medical examination. An appointment will then depend upon satisfactory references and a Criminal Record Bureau check.

Of course, no book explaining how to become a Fire Control Operator would be complete without teaching you what happens when a member of the public dials 999. So, without further ado, here's what happens:

Once a 999 call is made the caller will be answered by a Telephone Exchange Operator who will ask the caller which emergency service they require. The caller will be asked which service they require and once they are being connected to the Fire Service they will be able to hear the Telephone Exchange Operator passing their telephone number to the Fire Service Control Operator.

The Fire Service Control Operator will then ask the caller a number of questions as follows:

1. What is the full address? (It is at this stage that fire engines may be mobilised)

2. What is on fire?

3. Is there anybody trapped?

4. Are there any nearby landmarks?

5. What telephone number is the caller dialling from?

6. The caller may be asked for their name and address.

WHY DOES THE FIRE CONTROL OPERATOR NEED TO ASK YOU THESE QUESTIONS?

1. The FCOp needs to know the address where the emergency is. This information is entered into the computer to enable them to pinpoint exactly where their fire appliances need to attend.

2. They need to know what is on fire, or what other emergency the caller has to enable them to decide

what their response will be, i.e. how many fire engines they will send.

3. They need to know if people are trapped inside a building to enable the FCOp to offer fire survival advice.

4. Nearby landmarks, such as pubs or telephone boxes are valuable sources of information which enable the fire engine drivers to reach the location as quickly as possible.

5. They need to know the telephone number that the caller is calling from, so that they can contact them again if they need any further information from them. This information is not given to anyone other than emergency service personnel.

6. The FCOp may need to know the caller's name and address. This can be used as guidance to where the fire has been seen from.

TIP

For your FCOp interview, make sure you know what happens when a member of the public dials 999 and also the questions a Fire Control Operator asks and why.

Now let's take a look at a few frequently asked questions to give you more idea about the role of a Fire Control Operator.

FREQUENTLY ASKED QUESTIONS

Q. How old do you have to be to apply?

A. You must be aged 18 or over at the time of your application.

Q. What are the working hours?

A. The hours will certainly vary from Fire Service to Service and also with regards to how many shifts are adopted. However, as a general rule, the hours of a Fire Control Operator are run across two shift patterns:

1. 42 hour per week average across an eight week rota, comprised of two consecutive day duties (0700-1900), followed by two consecutive night duties (0900-1700). There are then four rest days.

2. 29 hours per week average across a five week rota, comprised of early shifts (0800-1500) and late shifts (1500-2200).

Q. Where will I be based?

A. Again, this depends on the service you are applying to join. Some Fire and Rescue Services still have their Fire Control based at the Fire and Rescue Service Headquarters, whereas others share their control room with other organisations such as the Police Force or Ambulance Service.

Q. What training will I receive?

A. The initial training is an intensive course which lasts for approximately five weeks and is classroom based. It includes both theory and practical application of skills. Once you join the overlay shift or one of the four 'watches', your training will continue to develop and improve your skills.

> **TIP**
>
> Find out the exact training you will undergo as a Fire Control Operator as this will likely be an interview question. The way to find out is to request a familiarisation visit to the Fire Control Centre prior to your interview.

Q. Is there a pension scheme?

A. Yes – You can contribute to the Local Government Pension Scheme.

Q. How much annual leave will I be entitled to?

A. Fire Control operators are entitled to 30 days annual leave each year. You will also receive a paid holiday on, or in respect of, public holidays.

Q. Will I have to wear a uniform?

A. Yes, a uniform is provided.

APPLICATION, TESTING & INTERVIEW ADVICE FOR FIRE CONTROL OPERATORS

APPLICATION

The application process has become more in-depth over recent years and Human Resources departments now favour the Personal Qualities and Attributes (PQA's) approach to assessment. This allows them to ensure that successful candidates have the right skills, qualities and experience to perform the role competently.

Within the application they will ask for examples of how you meet each of the PQA's that are within the application pack.

For example, one of the questions within the application form might say:

"Describe how you would see yourself as a team player and give an example of an occasion you have had to do this."

The best way to respond to this question is by describing an event that has involved you within that role. Write your response in a manner so that the person assessing your response has no idea about the subject, and by reading it they would understand the process fully what you are explaining. The more 'relevant' content you can put down in your response, the better, although do not 'waffle' in your response and also do not include irrelevant information. Applications with minimal input will be disregarded. Make sure you do your homework, go on the Fire Service's website and find out as much information as you can about the role and also the assessable PQA's. This will give you some understanding of the day-to-day running and expectations of the organisation you are trying to join.

 how2become

TESTING

Testing may vary from Fire Service to Fire Service; however, the tests will usually consist of the following three elements.

Audio Typing: this consists of listening to passages read out by an individual or from an audio recording device played out loud into the room. The aim of this test is to assess your typing speed, spelling, accuracy, listening skills and also your interpretation of what is being said. The content you provide will be examined, and even though you may not finish the passage, as long as the example is accurate and spelling is good this will be considered.

Word Comprehension: this is the ability to read text, process it and understand its meaning. This is tested by reading a passage that will then give a choice of the correct spelling and the meaning of the word. For example: "The presence of the man in the room" could also be written as "The presents of the man in the room." Both sound the same, but the written context is totally different.

Presence = the fact or condition of being present within your immediate surroundings or vicinity.

Presents = a gift or showing and giving, or an introduction.

Number Recall: this again, is either verbally given from a representative or a recording played in the room. A sequence of numbers is given; initially a lower set of numbers is given, i.e. **2928**. Then, as the test progresses, the length of sequence will increase i.e. **4935742**, and so on. You are required to write down the numbers in the correct sequence on your test paper. This test is used for listening and accuracy skills. Numbers are used to a high percentage of the working day within the role of an Operator and therefore, you need to demonstrate that your memory retention ability is high.

INTERVIEW

If you are accepted for interview following the tests, then you will be given an interview date and time. Arrive at least 15 minutes prior to your interview. This will show the assessors that you are prompt and good at time keeping, something which is crucial to the role of a Fire Control Operator as you need the time to carry out a concise and accurate handover before starting each shift.

Make sure you present yourself in a smart manner. A uniform is provided at the commencement of your role as a Fire Control Operator and this must always to be worn to an exact standard.

The interviews are usually held in front of a panel. This will normally consist of the Officer-in-Charge of the Control Room (Station or Group Manager Level), a Human Resources Representative, the Training Officer and at least one other Watch Manager. They will all have a list of PQA's in front of them, which will form the basis of the interview. They will ask you to give examples of how you have previously used the skills set out in the PQA document and also the person specification. They will also ask why you think you would be suitable for this type of role. They may also give you a scenario and then ask how you would deal with it. Remember that a great deal of the work within a Control Centre is Data Protected, so expect to be asked a question along those lines also. Here is a sample interview questions and response based on Data Protection:

Q. You are working as a Fire Control Operator and the local media call you the morning after a serious fire in which two people were seriously injured. The journalist asks you for the names and ages of those involved. How would you respond to the journalist?

A. *"To begin with, I would make sure I followed my training and guidance that is supplied by the Fire Service. If I were unsure about something I would ask my line manager. Having said that, I would never disclose any details under the Data Protection Act and certainly would not disclose the names or details of any individuals who were either directly or indirectly involved in an incident."*

Once the interview is completed, and if you are successful, you will then proceed to the Medical stage. A date and time will be given for this and attend, as before, promptly and in a smart manner.

MORE ABOUT THE ROLE AND LIFE OF A FIRE CONTROL OPERATOR

Within Emergency Fire Control there are four Watches. These are usually named as Red, Green, Blue or White Watch. They run in line with Station Watches, this enables a good relationship to be struck with Stations resulting in consistency between Station's and Control.

The shift pattern can consist of two × 9 hour day shifts, 0900 to 1800hrs and two × 15 hour night shifts, 1800 to 0900hrs, or in some cases two × 12 hour days and two × 12 hour night duties, running concurrently. Start times may vary depending on which part of the Country the Fire Service Control Room is based.

Each Watch consists of approximately seven/eight individuals, never going below five as a minimum. The rank structure would involve:

Watch Manager (WM) (Supervisor) × 1

Crew Managers (CM) × 2

Fire Control Operators – (FCOp) × 5

Almost all Control rooms work with three computers as follows:

The first computer is the Mobilizing 'live computer', or MOBs for short. This is the most important system you will work with. It is the system that sends all information to the Station's. As the Fire Position Operator it is the computer that you enter the relevant details into, such as location, type and equipment required for any incident that the Station's would attend. The MOBs system is connected to an electronic map and each appliance shows on that map using a separate number known as a 'Callsign'. The Appliance Callsign status will change on the map as soon as the Radio Operator types this into the MOBs. It is important to complete this function straight away as it can aid the Supervisor to see what is available for use and if the County is covered with appliances available in all locations.

The second computer is a standard PC, which is there for email, defect reporting, spreadsheets and holds all information from how to complete a defect form to what to send to more complicated incidents and how to complete/run them. This also includes Policies and the Fire and Rescue Service website.

The third computer is a touch screen telephone known as the Incident Command System (ICS) that has contacts to all the Station's, Outside Agencies such as Police, Ambulance, Gas and Electricity boards, Railways, Highways Agency etc.

> **As a FCOp the greatest skills you will require are:**
> **Communication and listening!**

Each rank sits at a desk and this in turn holds specific job roles for that day. These are handed out at change of shift/handover and it is vital that these are completed as soon as possible.

At the beginning of each shift you would 'take over' from the previous FCOp that has completed their shift. They will inform you of any incidents of interest or incidents that are still live and running; they may even ask you to contact outside agencies etc. to inform or gain information that is required for the incident. These are top priority and should be completed as soon as possible.

Once the handover is completed you will sign into each computer. The Fire position (999 line) and Radio positions will be the most involved positions of that shift.

All 999 incoming emergency calls will be routed to the Fire position and it is this person that will answer calls initially. Good listening skills and accurate, fast typing onto the Incident Format screen are essential. Once you become proficient in this you will usually have an appliance en-route to incident before you finish your call. If the incident is likely to be of a larger nature, or located on a motorway for instance, then numerous calls will be received and everyone else, apart from the Radio position, will answer calls.

The Radio position is where contact is continuously made with Fire Crews or Officers that are 'out and about' or in attendance at incidents; it is the main, mobile means of contact. Information is passed to the Radio Operator from the crews which is then typed onto the incident log, along with requests for further information or equipment they require. The information is confirmed with them, over the radio, that they are either **Mobile to incident, In Attendance or Mobile and Available**. Another Operator will already be

dealing with any requirements requested. This is also the method that a Fire Control Operator would pass onto the Crews any information that they felt was relevant, again this is all typed onto the incident log.

Appliances inform Control via Radio that they are available (which would indicate that they are available for reuse or redeployment). In this respect every appliance's whereabouts are known at all times.

Those FCOp's that are not sat at either the Fire or Radio positions, will sit at 'normal' positions. Each position has exactly the same equipment. These FCOp's would deal with general administrative calls, including some from Station's who need questions answered or if they are reporting defects on appliances etc.

On reporting defects it can require the appliance to be taken 'off the run' as they are not fit for service. This information must be passed onto the WM/CM so they can then determine if another appliance should be moved to that station. This issue would also require you to inform various people within the Service and all information annotated onto the system.

Stations will contact the Engineering Department themselves during weekday/daytime shifts. During night duties or weekends this will be Control's responsibility and an allocated Duty Engineer is contacted via a paging system or a phone call. They will nominate a Duty Mechanic to attend the defective appliance and it will be your responsibility to contact them and ensure that all the information is passed on. Once the appliance is back 'available' you must enter this back onto the MOBs; this ensures that the electronic map shows them being available. Informing the WM/CM is also essential so they can complete any actions they require to make.

At all times any information that you receive into Control is 'logged' whether it be on either the PC or MOBs or verbally passed onto your WM or CM.

Data protection is a huge part of your role as a Control Operator. During each shift duty you will encounter contact from the general Media, newspaper's, TV and radio. If there has been a particularly large or unusual incident, or sadly where someone has died or been injured during an incident, then these types of phone calls are to be expected. A statement from the Service Media Department will be passed to Control and only this is to be given. At no time do you mention names or full addresses and if callers are usually persistent then they would be passed through to the Media Department.

The following day each FCOp will move to the next position, and so on. This is to ensure that consistency on competency within each job role is completed enabling each FCOp to be able to complete any task that is asked of them. These are just a few examples of tasks that Fire Control complete on a daily basis.

Once your training is complete and you are on Watch, you are required to complete an electronic training system. This will help to keep you up-to-date with all of your newly acquired skills. This job is one that has an ongoing learning process as policies and procedures are continuously changing and being updated. You will be expected to check these daily. Some information you gain via the electronic training system is essential, especially if it affects a certain aspect of mobilizing to an incident.

Ongoing training is completed on a daily basis with specific topics depicted monthly. You would be nominated a Mentor who is usually a Crew Manager. They will monitor your

progress and appraise you at six monthly intervals. Watch training is completed either on a written questions and answers basis or via a practical exercise that your Mentor will arrange. These usually consist of scenario's dealing with more complicated attendances to incidents i.e. Chemical, Marine or Air incidents. This can be completed where there is a gap in the day that you are not so busy or on your night duties. It is important that these records are kept up-to-date and will need to be completed on a daily basis. This will secure your 'competency payment' that you receive each month, once you are a qualified, competent Fire Control Operator.

The whole process of becoming qualified/competent depends on each Fire Service; however, as an example, the whole process usually takes one to two years.

WHAT TYPE OF INCIDENTS DOES THE FIRE SERVICE RESPOND TO?

In this next section of the guide I want explain some of the different type of incidents the Fire Service attends on a daily basis. This information will be great preparation for your interview.

> **TIP**
>
> Be aware of the type of incidents the Fire Service attends. You may get asked what they are at interview.

Accidental dwelling fires

This type of fire is exactly as it says – accidental. Somebody in the home may have started a fire by accident. For example, somebody may return from the pub late at night and decide

they want to grill some food. Unfortunately, the effects of alcohol or even drugs can send people to sleep and help them to forget the important aspect of safety. Before they know it they are awoken by the sound of a smoke alarm (providing they have one fitted) and a serious fire in the kitchen caused by unattended food left under the grill or even a chip pan.

NEVER pour water onto a burning chip pan. This is one of the key messages that Firefighters tell the public time and time again.

There are a number of different ways in which accidental dwelling fires can occur:

- Faulty electrical goods or wiring that has not been tested or maintained;

- Overloaded electrical sockets;

- Cooking left unattended;

- Chimney fires as a result of the chimney or flue not being cleaned.

Deliberate fires

Deliberate fires are the most common fires that you will mobilize firefighters to. These can vary in degree and type and are a constant problem for Fire Services up and down the country. These can range from a small bin fire in a high street or park, which has been set alight deliberately, or even a stolen car that has been set alight to hide any forensic evidence. Examples of deliberate fires are set out below:

Deliberate rubbish fires

This type of fire usually occurs where a quantity of rubbish has been left out by the occupier of a shop, home or business. If you drive around in your car or walk around the

street, you will be able to see rubbish carelessly discarded. This is a potential target for the arsonist and you will mobilize firefighters to many fires of this nature.

Deliberate car/vehicle fires
Sometimes car thieves and joy riders steal cars for various reasons. You will almost certainly find yourself mobilizing firefighters to car fires in the middle of the night involving vehicles that have been stolen, abandoned and set alight. This type of fire can be particularly hazardous due to the chemicals, foams and other complex materials used in the manufacture of vehicles.

Chemical incidents
This type of incident is especially dangerous and hazardous to the firefighter. As a Fire Control Operator you will mobilize firefighters and officers to incidents that involve the spillage, mishandling, careless disposal or discovery of an unknown or potentially dangerous substance.

You will find that each individual Fire Service has its own operational procedures for dealing with this type of incident.

Road Traffic Collisions (RTCs)
Every year, hundreds of people die in car accidents up and down the country. It is an unfortunate fact that people still speed, drink and drive, or drive without due care and attention. Although modern safety standards have improved massively over recent years, some people's attitudes to the roads have not.

You will mobilize firefighters to incidents of an unpleasant nature where casualties are often trapped in a vehicle as a result of a collision or accident. This type of work requires untold professional skill from the firefighter to carefully extract

the person trapped inside. As you can imagine, as a Fire Control Operator you will have to deal with distressing calls where people are reporting RTC's. It will be your job to calm the caller down before extracting really important information, such as details of casualties and the all-important location of the incident.

During RTC's, firefighters operate machinery, operated by hydraulic methods, which has the capability of moving great weights in any direction and is designed to help them create space in which to work, so the casualty can be freed without further injury. Some of the equipment firefighters use whilst attending this type of incident is extremely versatile and powerful and is often carried on specialist appliances, which you will be required to mobilize at a moment's notice.

You will find that you need to work closely with the police and ambulance crews when mobilizing to these types of incidents. You will also have to liaise with the Highways Agency to inform them of incidents and road closures etc.

Animal rescues

There will certainly be times when you mobilize crews to rescue a trapped or injured animal from a variety of situations. You will certainly mobilize crews to cows or horses that have become stuck in mud or have found their way into ponds, lakes, rivers or canals and cannot get out. The difficulty in this type of situation is that the animal usually does not want to be rescued and is fearful of the team trying to rescue it.

Once again, specialist teams are trained to deal with these incidents and you will need to know the whereabouts and location of the specialist Animal Rescue Units within your county area.

Personal Protective Equipment (PPE)

As with all jobs where a hazard or risk is involved, firefighters wear protective clothing. Within the Fire Service this is more commonly known as Personal Protective Equipment (PPE) and covers a wide range of clothing and equipment from fire tunics, gloves, boots and helmets, to breathing apparatus, safety glasses and impact shields.

When a firefighter joins the Fire Service and becomes a fire-fighter, they will be issued with their own Personal Protective Equipment, which includes fire boots, protective tunic and leggings, firefighting gloves, a flash-hood and a helmet.

Fire tunics and leggings

These form the main body of the firefighter's protection and cover the main torso or body area. They are always made of fabric containing fire resistant qualities of varying grades and must meet specific standards in relation to protection. Not all Fire Services have the same style of uniform or colour. For example, firefighters from Essex wear the colour gold, which is a more unconventional colour of PPE. This colour is highly reflective in a fire and affords great protection. More common colours include blue and black.

Gloves, boots and helmet

To provide firefighters with full protection, they are required to wear gloves, boots and a helmet whilst attending the majority of operational incidents that you will mobilize them to. Once again, these must meet stringent regulations in relation to build quality, design and safety. Each Fire Service will buy different types and styles depending on their individual budgets and requirements.

Flash-hood

This is an extremely important part of the firefighter's uniform and must always be worn whilst attending incidents. The flash-hood protects the main head portion and neck from heat, fire and flame. It is designed specifically to withstand high temperatures and will provide you with a certain amount of protection when fighting fires both internally and externally. Firefighters wear flash-hoods to protect themselves from flash burns and scalds.

Breathing apparatus

Breathing apparatus (BA) is used by firefighters when entering a building or premises to tackle a fire. It can also be used externally when tackling car fires or barn fires to provide 'comfort' to the wearer and prevent him or her from breathing in the toxic fumes or smoke. Many years ago firefighters only 'donned' breathing apparatus as a last resort, whereas now it is seen as a vital part of the firefighter's PPE.

The breathing apparatus set consists of a harness configuration, which incorporates adjustable straps to give the wearer maximum comfort. It will also contain a cylinder, usually of a lightweight construction, containing compressed air that the user will draw on through the facemask.

There are usually four sets of breathing apparatus to each fire engine.

THE ROLE STRUCTURE WITHIN THE FIRE SERVICE

As a Fire Control Operator you will need to be aware of the different roles each person plays within the Fire Service. Each position along the chain holds a level of responsibility, which will vary according to the Fire Service that you decide to join.

A brief description of each role is outlined below:

CONTROL ROOM STAFF

Fire Control Operators
They answer the 999 calls, send out fire engines and provide incident support and access to specialist information.

Crew Manager
They provide first line supervision of all calls being received and fire engines sent. They also deputise for the Watch Manager.

Watch Manager
The Watch Manager is responsible for managing the operational efficiency and performance of the Watch, along with welfare support and monitoring.

OPERATIONAL FIREFIGHTERS AND MANAGERS

Firefighter
Responsible for operational firefighting duties and responding to incidents as required. They are also responsible for carrying out Community Fire Safety work as required. Within some Fire Service organisations firefighters are sometimes given the option to work in specific specialised fields such as Technical Fire Safety.

Crew Manager
Usually the person in charge of a fire appliance but, again, he or she may work in other specialised areas.

Watch Manager
Watch Managers can be either in charge of a watch or a fire appliance. They can also work in specialised roles such as Technical Fire Safety or Community Fire Safety.

Station Manager

Station Managers can be the person in charge of a watch, a fire station, or even a group of fire stations depending on the Fire Service in question. Technical Fire Safety Inspecting Officers usually hold this role also. Once again, the Station Manager may work in a specialised role away from operational duties.

Group Manager

Group Managers are usually responsible for a group of fire stations or a division/area.

Area Manager

Area Managers are usually responsible for a division or a large area.

Assistant Chief Fire Officer

The Assistant to the Chief Fire Officer may also be responsible for a large area or division.

Chief Fire Officer/Brigade Manager

This is the person who has overall responsibility for the management of the Fire Service. He or she will be responsible to the County Council or Local Authority for the efficient running of the Fire Service.

NETWORKING FOR WOMEN IN THE FIRE SERVICE (NWFS)

In 1993, the NWFS was established as a self-help group for women in the Fire and Rescue Service. Over recent years, NWFS has sought to influence the equality agenda, engaging with the major players in order to ensure the voice of all women in the Fire and Rescue Service is heard.

NWFS is an independent voluntary group of people who aim to contribute to making the Fire and Rescue Service a place

where women and men can work together harmoniously and professionally, and to contribute to developing a thriving Fire and Rescue Service that supports and actively encourages women in achieving their full potential within the Service.

The aim of NWFS

- Ensuring that the Fire and Rescue Service consistently demonstrates that it values women;

- Contributing to achieving a gender, ethnicity and sexual orientation balance across the rank and role structure consistent with the proportion of women in the active population;

- Having a voice in influencing policy;

- Having a working environment and equipment of the right quality and standards in order to enable women to undertake their role;

- Developing an understanding of the competing demands in achieving a work/life balance and fulfilling role.

To find out more about Networking for Women in the Fire Service please visit: www.nwfs.net.

EQUALITY AND FAIRNESS IN THE FIRE SERVICE

Equality and fairness is a very important subject and one that you should be familiar with when you apply to join the Fire Service. Under the Race Relations (Amendment) Act, public authorities (including the Fire and Rescue Service) have a general duty to promote race equality. This means that when carrying out their functions or duties they must have due regard to the need to:

- Eliminate unlawful discrimination;

- Promote equality of opportunity;

- Promote good relations between persons of different racial groups.

In order to demonstrate how a Fire and Rescue Service plan to meet their statutory duties, they have an obligation to produce and publish what is called a Race Equality Scheme.

The Race Equality Scheme outlines their strategy and action plan to ensure that equality and diversity are mainstreamed through their policies, practices, procedures and functions. Central to this strategy are external consultation, monitoring and assessment, training, and ensuring that the public has access to this information.

It is advised that you are aware of the Race Equality Scheme for the individual Fire Service that you are applying to join. By doing this, you will have learnt a considerable amount about this important topic before you join the Fire Service and also, more importantly, you will hopefully demonstrate a commitment to Equality and Fairness. Read, digest and understand the following statement:

"Equality is not about treating everybody the same, but recognising we are all individuals, unique in our own way. Equality and fairness is about recognising, accepting and valuing people's unique individuality according to their needs. This often means that individuals may be treated appropriately, yet fairly, based on their needs."

CHAPTER TWO

THE FIRE CONTROL OPERATOR JOB DESCRIPTION AND PERSON SPECIFICATION

This short chapter of the guide is, in my opinion, one of the most important ones to take on-board during your preparation, if you are to have any chance of passing the selection process.

One of the first things you need to do before you submit your application for the role is to obtain the person specification and job description. These two important documents will tell you what the assessors are looking for from candidates during each stage of the selection process. If you know what they are looking for, then you have far greater chance of succeeding.

I can also safely say that it is possible to predict the interview

questions from the information contained within these two documents. To begin with, take a look at the following example person specification for the role of Fire Control operator:

PERSON SPECIFICATION

Job Title: Fire Control Operator

Dept: Fire Control

Requirements	Essential	Desirable	How Measured (see key below)
EXPERIENCE/KNOWLEDGE			
• Data Input experience		✓	A, T, I
• Audio Typing experience		✓	A, T, I
• Experience with two way frequency radio systems		✓	A, I
• Topographical knowledge of the area		✓	A, I
• Previous experience of working with the public		✓	A, I
SKILLS/COMPETENCE			
• Good verbal and written communication skills	✓		A, T, I
• Retentive memory	✓		T
• Computer literate	✓		A, T
• Good telephone skills	✓		A, T

EDUCATION/TRAINING

• Good level of literacy and numeracy skills	✓		T, P
• Typing or computer studies qualification		✓	A, P
• Willingness to undergo continual learning	✓		I

PERSONAL ATTRIBUTES

• Work calmly under pressure	✓		T, R
• Flexible and adaptable	✓		A, I
• Ability to work as part of a team	✓		A, I

OTHER RELEVANT (JOB SPECIFIC) POINTS

• Commitment to Equality and Diversity	✓		A,I
• Commitment to Health and Safety	✓		A
• Must be prepared to work shifts including nights, weekends and public holidays	✓		I

A = Application, T = Test, I = Interview, R = References, P = Proof (certificates etc.)

You will note on the form that there are both ESSENTIAL and DESIRABLE criteria. It is your job to make sure you absolutely meet the ESSENTIAL criteria and try your hardest to match as many DESIRABLE criteria as possible. The more

DESIRABLES you meet, the greater chance of success you will have. You will also note that, in the right hand column, you are made aware of the method of assessment for each particular area with the key to each letter indicated at the foot of the specification. This means you have the knowledge to predict when you will be required to provide details and evidence of where you meet each ESSENTIAL and DESIRABLE criteria.

If, when shortlisting, there are a high volume of candidates who meet the essential criteria, there may be a need for the recruitment staff to narrow the field or distinguish between candidates. Therefore, candidates may need to meet DESIRABLE criteria to be considered eligible for employment. That is why I encourage you to meet as many desirables as possible during your preparation.

Based on the above, the following ESSENTIALS and DESIRABLES are going to be assessed at interview:

- Data Input experience
- Audio Typing experience
- Experience with two way frequency radio systems
- Topographical knowledge of the area
- Previous experience of working with the public
- Good verbal and written communication skills
- Willingness to undergo continual learning
- Flexible and adaptable
- Ability to work as part of a team
- Commitment to Equality and Diversity
- Must be prepared to work shifts including nights, weekends and public holidays

The way to demonstrate that you meet each of these assessable areas is to prepare yourself for the following interview questions:

Q1. What current data input experience do you have and how do you go about inputting data when required?

TIP: Prior to your interview make sure you have obtained sufficient data inputting experience. You may also decide to attend a data inputting course through an accredited training provider such as www.pitman-training.com.

Q2. What audio typing experience do you have?

TIP: Prior to your interview make sure you have obtained sufficient audio typing experience. You may also decide to attend an audio transcription course through an accredited training provider such as www.pitman-training.com.

Q3. Can you give an example of when you have worked with two-way frequency radio systems?

TIP: Of course, most people who apply to become a Fire Control Operator will have little or no experience of two-way frequency radio systems. If you fall in to this category, my advice would be to try and arrange a familiarisation visit at your local Fire Control Centre. During your visit ask the Fire Control Operators to explain what two-way frequency radio systems are and how they fit in to the role of a Fire Control Operator. The following information may also be useful for you to relay to the interviewer if they ask a question of this nature:

"A two-way radio is a radio that can both transmit and receive (a transceiver), unlike a broadcast receiver which only receives content. A two-way radio (transceiver) allows the operator to have a conversation with other similar radios operating on the same radio frequency (channel). Two-way radios are available in mobile, stationary base and hand-held

portable configurations. Hand-held radios are often called walkie-talkies or just hand-helds.

Two-way radio systems usually operate in a half-duplex mode; that is, the operator can talk, or he can listen, but not at the same time. A push-to-talk or Press To Transmit button activates the transmitter; when it is released the receiver is active. A mobile phone or cellular telephone is an example of a two-way radio that both transmits and receives at the same time (called full-duplex mode). It uses two different radio frequencies (channels) to carry the two directions of the conversation simultaneously."

Q4. What does the term 'topography' mean and also what is your topographical knowledge like of the county area?

In very basic terms, topography is the detailed mapping or charting of the features of a relatively small area, district, or locality. Although this is a DESIRABLE, according to our sample job description, this is one area that you can gain extra marks during the interview. As I mentioned during the early stages of the guide, write down and learn all of the key risks and landmarks within the county area that you are applying to become a Fire Control Operator. These might include:

- Major roads and motorways
- Large industrial centres or areas
- Power plants
- Buildings and areas of special interest
- Rivers or lakes that hold large volumes of water

Q5. Do you have any previous experience of working with the public?

If you do not have any previous experience, consider carrying out some charity work prior to applying for the role of a Fire

Control Operator. This is a good way to demonstrate that you have the ability to work within your local community.

Q6. Can you give an example of when you have learnt a new or existing skill?

Having a specific answer to this question will demonstrate to the interview panel that you are willing to undergo continual learning, something that is integral to the role of a Fire Control Operator.

Q7. Are you prepared to work weekends, bank holidays and shift patterns? Can you give examples of when you have previously worked in these types of situation?

Being flexible and adaptable is crucial to the role. Make sure you have some experience in this type of situation.

Q8. Can you give an example of when you have worked as part of a team?

A willingness to work as part of a team is vital to the role. See the interview section of this guide for a sample answer to this question.

Q9. Can you give an example of when you have challenged someone's actions that were either discriminatory or inappropriate?

A commitment to equality and diversity is very important in the Fire Service. This will be assessed in detail during the interview. See the interview section for a sample response to this type of question. Above all, make sure you believe in equality and diversity.

Hopefully you are now beginning to learn how to match the assessable areas during each stage of the selection process. As you can see from the above tutorial, it is certainly possible to predict the interview questions from the person specification!

Now let's take a look at a sample job description and how we can use this to further prepare ourselves for selection.

FIRE AND RESCUE SERVICE
Job Description

Job Title:	Fire Control Operator
Directorate:	Community Protection - Control
Responsible to:	Watch Manager / Crew Manager
Location:	Command and Control Centre

Purpose of the job: To be capable of efficiently dealing with all emergency calls and mobilising the appropriate response.

Context of the role:

- The Fire and Rescue Service work towards protecting life and property and providing a quality Fire Safety Service.

- The Command and Control Centre forms part of the Community Protection Directorate within the Service and comprises of twenty-six members of staff. It is responsible for handling all emergency calls, determining correct resources, mobilising and providing all support assistance.

- The Fire Control Operator is a member of the Implementation Group: Operational Delivery, they contribute to effective implementation of policies and procedures.

- The Fire Control Operator operates within a framework provided by the Service's Business Plans, operational policies and procedures. On a day-to-day basis the post holder is responsible for receiving emergency calls from members of the public and mobilising appliances to incidents.

- The Service expects the highest standard of communication and conduct from all staff. Respect for confidentiality is essential.

- All staff are expected to participate positively in the Appraisal Process, to undertake relevant training and development activities to improve their work performance, and to contribute to the training and development of others.

- To promote the Service's policy of equality and fairness, both within the Service and externally in order to demonstrate commitment to anti discriminatory practice in all the Services' activities.

- To practice and promote the health and safety policies of the Service. To contribute to the development and progression of health and safety within the sphere of responsibility of this role for all employees and service recipients.

- The areas of responsibility associated with a particular post may be amended from time to time, and it is expected that the post holder will operate flexibly within the role, location of the role and undertake any other tasks and projects which could reasonably be expected of someone holding this role.

KEY RESPONSIBILITIES AND DUTIES

1. To handle efficiently all types of emergency calls and mobilising the appropriate appliances promptly.

2. To handle all routine administrative calls.

3. To efficiently operate the Services Mobilising System.

4. To efficiently operate the Services Communication System and all associated equipment.

5. To be able to operate, to varying extents, the Management Information System as directed by the Watch Manager.

6. To efficiently operate all other equipment within the Control Room.

7. To assist the Training and Support Manager as directed by the Watch Manager, in line with current agreements.

8. To undertake central progressive or specialised Control related training as and when required.

9. To serve as Fire Control Operator on any watch or in any Control related post as directed by the Chief Executive commensurate with your Contract of Employment.

10. To undertake any further duties as may be required, which are commensurate with the post.

During the interview your knowledge and understanding of the job description will allow you to answer some of the questions with high marks. As you can see from the job description, it clearly lays out both the context for the role and also the key responsibilities and duties. By learning the job description you will be able to answer the following two interview questions:

Q. What do you understand about the role of a Fire Control Operator and what do they do on a day-to-day basis?

Q. What are the key duties and responsibilities of a Fire Control Operator?

Unless you study and learn both the job description and person specification, you are highly likely to fail at the interview. Make sure you obtain a copy of both of them and also be able to provide evidence of where you meet the essentials and desirables for the role.

Let's now take a look at the application form so that you have a thorough understanding of how to complete it accurately.

CHAPTER THREE

THE FIRE CONTROL OPERATOR APPLICATION FORM

The application form is an important part of the recruitment process. The information you provide on the application form enables the Fire Service recruitment team to decide whether or not you are shortlisted for testing and for interview. The form is also used as the basis for the interview itself.

Before you start to complete the application form, read the job description/role profile, candidate specification, which details the essential/desirable qualities of the post holder. Ensure that you fully complete the application, covering all the requirements detailed on the candidate specification. Do not assume that the assessors have knowledge of your experience and skills; tell them about your experience and skills as they are unable to guess or make assumptions. If you need any assistance in completing the application form

due to a disability, then make sure you let the Fire Service know and they will be more than happy to help you.

COMPLETING THE APPLICATION FORM

The following guidance will assist you in completing your application form. I want to stress from the outset that the some Fire and Rescue Services will now require you to complete an online application. The information I have provided which follows is aimed at both online forms and also paper-based ones, too.

JOB TITLE AND DETAILS

The post title and post reference number will be in the advert for the post and will usually be available to select in the online application form. However, if they are not available make sure you find out the reference number as you will need this when completing the application.

SCREENING QUESTIONS

Sometimes, Fire and Rescue Services will ask a series of screening questions to highlight key requirements of your prospective employment as a Fire Control Operator. For example, all employees are required to have permission to work in the UK, either through nationality or the Border Agency. The FCOp role will also require you to work unsociable hours and this question may be asked during the initial screening process.

EDUCATION, QUALIFICATIONS AND TRAINING

When completing the form you may be required to give details of your education and qualifications obtained throughout your education. This includes any qualifications which you are studying at the time of your application. Details of recent/relevant training courses should also be given within this section. I mentioned earlier about a number of courses you may wish to attend through an accredited training provider. This would be the ideal time to add these course qualifications in this section. If you are invited for interview you will be asked to produce proof of any relevant qualification(s) e.g. your certificate(s).

PRESENT/MOST RECENT EMPLOYMENT/ PREVIOUS EMPLOYMENT OR VOLUNTARY WORK

This section tells the assessors about your previous employment record, providing a brief description of the duties and responsibilities of the job. Make sure you include all jobs whether full time/ temporary/ part time/ voluntary or any periods of self-employment. This will also be a great place to add any charity or unpaid work you have carried out. Employment dates should be continuous and if you have had any gaps in employment, you need to tell them why; i.e. a career break, a period of studying, caring for children or parents, unemployment, etc.

With the "Reason for Leaving / Wishing to Leave" section, be careful what you put. A positive reason for leaving or wanting to leave a job might be:

"I am seeking to find a new and fresh challenge which will push me and allow me to learn and implement new skills. I am also looking for a new role which will enable me to work within the local community."

In the **Brief Description of Duties** question I strongly advise that you try to match some of the duties that are required to become a competent Fire Control Operator as detailed in the person specification. These might include:

- Communicating effectively with customers both verbally and also in writing.

- Dealing with telephone calls professionally and promptly in order to resolve questions and queries.

- Being flexible in my role and also being available to work unsociable hours as and when required.

- Working as part of a team in order to complete company tasks and goals.

- Inputting data and information into computer systems in line with my training.

- Audio typing information that has been relayed by customers over the phone into our online logging system.

- Being able to retain by memory details of customers' orders during telephone conversations and then passing this information over accurately to the warehouse despatch team.

- Dealing with pressurised situations including remaining calm under pressure whilst dealing with customer complaints etc.

- Managing my own professional development by carrying out online company training programmes and keeping my personal development log up-to-date.

Of course, you cannot be dishonest when completing the application form and you can only detail duties that you actually have performed in a current or previous role. However, the above list will give you an idea of types of duties that will help you to gain higher marks when completing the application form.

COMPETENCY BASED QUESTIONS

These questions are based on the candidate specification and are designed to focus your knowledge, skills and experience on key aspects of the role. There is sometimes also an open section for you to provide the application form assessors with clear examples on how your skills, knowledge or experience meet the needs of the job. As already explained, the person specification and job description will give you an idea of what the assessors are looking for. The question on the form that relates to this part of the assessment might read:

Q. Describe how you meet the selection criteria as defined in the person specification for the role.

EMPLOYMENT REFERENCES

At some point you will be required to provide details of at least one reference who can give the Fire Service an assessment of your suitability for the post of Fire Control Operator. Personal references are not acceptable. Also, check in advance with your referee that they are happy to be contacted for a reference. If you are currently employed, your referee must be your current employer. If currently unemployed, your referee should be your most recent employer.

DISCLOSING CRIMINAL CONVICTIONS

Certain criminal convictions are 'spent' (forgotten) after a rehabilitation period and you are unlikely to need to inform the Fire Service about these during your application. I would encourage you to confirm this information by visiting the Fire Service website you are applying to join.

DRIVING QUALIFICATIONS

Although most Fire and Rescue Services do not make it mandatory to have a full driving licence in order to become a Fire Control Operator, you need to be certain that you can actually get to work each day. Having a full UK driving licence will be an advantage to your application as a Fire Control Operator.

On the following pages I have provided you with a sample paper-based application form to give you a better understanding of what it might look like and the questions asked. Following the sample application form I will provide you with a response to the competency-based question to assist you when completing your form.

PART ONE

1. CURRENT / MOST RECENT EMPLOYMENT

Name and Address of Current or Most Recent Employer

Post title

Date Employment Commenced (and terminated if appropriate)

Current Salary

Employer's Business / Industry

Period of Notice

Brief Description of Duties

Reason for Leaving / Wishing to Leave

2. EMPLOYMENT HISTORY

As part of our commitment to safeguarding practices for children, young people and vulnerable adults, you are required to provide details of any gaps in your working history.

Previous Employer (most recent first)	Dates of Employment From / To	Job Title and Main Duties	Reason for Leaving

3. QUALIFICATIONS AND TRAINING

Please give details of all educational qualifications you have obtained from school, college, university, etc.

Name of Educational Establishment	Subject and Qualifications Obtained	Dates of Study	Grade Achieved

4. MEMBERSHIP OF PROFESSIONAL BODIES

Name of Body/Qualification	Class/Grade of Membership

5. WORK RELATED COURSES/TRAINING

Please give details of any courses you have attended which are particularly relevant to the role (continue on pages provided at the end of this form if required).

Course Title/ Subject	Organising Body	Dates Attended	Duration of Course (e.g. 1 day)

6. SKILLS AND EXPERIENCE RELEVANT TO THE POST

Describe how you meet the selection criteria as defined in the person specification for the role.

Continue on separate sheet if required

PART TWO

Candidate Number
(Office Use Only)

---

7. POST APPLIED FOR

Post title

Closing Date

8. EQUAL OPPORTUNITIES MONITORING QUESTIONNAIRE

Completion of this section of the application form will help us to ensure equality of opportunity. Please note: **This information forms no part of the recruitment process. It will be detached from your application on receipt.**

Gender   MALE ☐   FEMALE ☐   **Date of Birth** .... / .... / ....

Age Group 17-24 ☐   25-35 ☐   36-45 ☐   46-55 ☐   56-65 ☐   66+ ☐

Ethnic Origin (tick as appropriate)

White
☐ British
☐ Irish
☐ Any other white background

Mixed
☐ White and Black Caribbean
☐ White and Black African
☐ White and Asian
☐ Any other mixed background

Asian or Asian British
☐ Indian
☐ Pakistani
☐ Bangladeshi
☐ Any other Asian background

Black or Black British
☐ Caribbean
☐ African
☐ Any other Black background

Chinese
☐ Chinese

Other ethnic group
☐ Any other (please specify);

☐ Prefer not to specify

Would you describe yourself as having a disability?   YES ☐   NO ☐

(Please note: This information is required for monitoring and also to ensure that if you require adjustments for the interview we can facilitate this. The Equality Act defines a disability as a physical or mental impairment which has a substantial long term adverse effect on a person's ability to carry out normal day to day activities).

Do you have any specific requirements to enable you to fully participate in the recruitment process?   YES ☐   NO ☐   If Yes, please provide details below:

Sexual Orientation (tick as appropriate)

☐ Bisexual   ☐ Gay / Lesbian
☐ Heterosexual   ☐ Prefer not to say

Religious Belief / Faith (tick as appropriate)

☐ Buddhist   ☐ Christian
☐ Hindu   ☐ Jewish
☐ Muslim   ☐ Sikh
☐ None   ☐ Other (please state)
☐ Prefer not to say

How did you hear of this vacancy? (tick as appropriate)

☐ Advert in Press   ☐ Fire Service   ☐ Poster in the
   (please specify)   Employee   community
                                                          (please specify)

☐ Website   ☐ Careers Adviser   ☐ Local Fire Station
   (please specify)   (please specify)

☐ Strategic Partner   ☐ Job Centre   ☐ Community
                                                        Engagement Event
                                                        (please specify)

☐ Other (please specify)

---

9. DRIVING QUALIFICATIONS

The answer to the following question will only be taken into consideration during the selection process if driving is an essential requirement of the job for which you are applying.

Do you hold a Full UK driving licence?   YES ☐   NO ☐

If NO, please indicate your driving qualifications, i.e. Non Driver, Provisional Licence, Penalty Points with dates etc.

10. PERSONAL DETAILS

Last or Family Name . . . .

First Name(s) . . . .

Permanent Address: . . . .

. . . .

Town . . . . County . . . . Post code . . . .

Telephone No (Home): . . . .

Telephone No (Mobile): . . . .

E-Mail address (if applicable): . . . .

National Insurance Number _____/_____/____/_____/____

Are you eligible to live and work in the UK according to the
Asylum and Immigration Act 2006   YES ☐   NO ☐

If No, please detail

. . . .

. . . .

Are you able to produce original documentation to confirm this right?

                                    YES ☐   NO ☐

11. REFERENCES

NB appointment will only be confirmed subject to satisfactory references.

Reference 1	Reference 2
Name	Name
. . . .	. . . .
Position/Title	Position/Title
. . . .	. . . .
Address	Address
. . . .	. . . .
Post Code	Post Code
. . . .	. . . .
Telephone No	Telephone No
. . . .	. . . .
E-Mail Address	E-Mail Address
. . . .	. . . .
Relationship	Relationship
. . . .	. . . .
i.e. employer, tutor, character referee	i.e. employer, tutor, character referee

12. DECLARATION OF CONVICTIONS

Do you have any unspent convictions?   YES ☐   NO ☐
If yes please detail below:

Offences	Date of conviction	Judgement and sentence

Any additional information (including "spent" convictions where the role requires this – see Person Specification)

13. GENERAL DECLARATION

I agree to the information in this form being stored for the purposes of my application, for monitoring and for reasonable research into the application process, in accordance with the Data Protection Act. I confirm that I have completed this application form and that to the best of my knowledge the information I have provided in it is true, accurate and correct.

Signed ....   Date ....

Please note: Approaching any elected Councillor or employee of a Fire Authority directly or indirectly to promote this application or providing false/misleading information in this application form shall disqualify you from appointment or if appointed may render you liable to disciplinary action, which could lead to your dismissal.

I will now provide you with a sample response to the all-important competency based application form question. This will give you a good idea as to how to structure your own response to this question.

Q. Describe how you meet the selection criteria as defined in the person specification for the role.

I believe I have the skills, qualities and attributes to become a competent member of the Fire Control team. To begin with, I have vast experience of communicating with members of the public, both verbally and also in writing. This experience was gained whilst working as a call centre operator for a large telecommunications company. Within this role I was required to answer a large quantity of telephone calls professionally and promptly in order to resolve questions and queries. I had set targets to meet each hour. During the calls I would have to remember the customer's details before inputting them into the company computer data system. This level of audio typing was an essential part of my role and during my last appraisal I was praised for my consistency in this area as I made zero mistakes for the quarter. I am also very much used to working under pressure. Every day I would deal with dissatisfied customers and it was my job to calm them down, extract the information required from them as fast as possible, before deciding upon the correct course of action in order to resolve their issues.

Flexibility within a role has always been second nature to me. I have worked in a shift environment for over 3 years now and during this time I would often volunteer to work weekends or additional hours to help the company. To that end, I am a highly motivated and dedicated team player who understands how important it is to work towards a company's goals and mission. Finally, I can be relied upon to look after and maintain my own continuous professional development as I have been doing this for 3 years now within my current role.

I strongly believe that I have the potential to become a competent Fire Control Operator and would very much appreciate the opportunity to progress to the next stages of selection.

SAMPLE RESPONSES TO PERSON SPECIFICATION CRITERIA ON THE APPLICATION FORM

Some Fire and Rescue Services will ask a series of competency-based questions on the application form. I will now offer you a number of sample responses based on anticipated criteria values relevant to the role.

PLEASE NOTE: The following responses are also great to use during the FCOp interview.

Criteria: Demonstrate outstanding communication skills, both written and verbal. Candidates must possess the ability to quickly establish both the customer needs and the nature of the Fire Service response required.

Response: My current role as a customer services call handler requires me to answer incoming calls from customers who have received faulty or incorrect products in response to orders they placed. As part of my role, I must remain calm and listen carefully to their complaints, while also being assertive if I feel they are particularly unhappy with the situation. I must also observe customer policy and focus on providing a positive experience for the customer. I had to speak to my line manager yesterday about a customer who had been waiting 2 weeks for a product. By communicating well with the customer I was able to deliver excellent customer service and offered my sincere apologies for the poor service received. He received the product the next day, together with some vouchers to spend in a well-known retail store and a 10% discount on his next order.

Criteria: Demonstrate an excellent ability to listen and subsequently interpret information before conducting an accurate risk assessment based on the information provided.

Response: I was asked to deal with a particularly distressed customer who felt that the product she had received wasn't as described when she made her order. By listening to her concerns and how she described making the original order, I realised that she had made a mistake during the ordering process and clicked onto the wrong product. I explained what I thought she had done, advised her not to worry, as I understand the website can be misleading if you are not used to it and rectified the situation. This prevented a customer complaint – against which my department is assessed – and the customer was very happy with the result. She eventually wrote a letter of thanks for my patience and ability to resolve the situation.

Criteria: Show resilience in pressured situations, especially when dealing with stressful situations and often extremely emotional customers

Response: I had an experience of this situation earlier this month in my position within the Customer Feedback Department. One customer had ordered a gift for his terminally ill wife which arrived three weeks later than we had originally indicated. Unfortunately, during that time she passed away. The customer was extremely distressed by both the late delivery and also the fact that we had contacted his late wife for customer service feedback. I apologised sincerely and arranged for the company to collect the gift from the customer and also to refund the money to his account with an additional £10 as a gesture of apology. As the funeral was still to take place, the company sent a note of condolence and a wreath to the service. The customer later rang and thanked me for my understanding at a difficult time.

Criteria: Ability to make decisions quickly and appropriately based on the information provided.

Response: This actually happened while I worked in the design department of my previous employer. I was required to proof read a client's brochure after it had gone to print and found a typing error in the content. I had to make a quick decision on what to do as this was our most important client. My manager was on holiday so I was the only person available to make a decision. I cancelled the print run before it was completed pending the corrections. It did cost the department money it had not budgeted for but less than it would have done for the whole of the print run. My supervisor was relieved that I used my initiative and the client was very happy with the overall product.

Criteria: Demonstrate an ability to work effectively within a team and a willingness to support their colleagues in achieving their goals.

Response: I currently work as a business analyst carrying out telephone surveys with my clients. Last month we were asked to provide a proposal for a project with a new client. The person normally responsible for it was overseas on business so I agreed to help, working overtime for two weeks to ensure we obtained all the relevant information to be successful in the proposal. We were ultimately awarded the contract and I received a small bonus for helping out.

Criteria: Show an adaptability to both learn and retain relevant information.

Response: In my role as Telesales Manager, I was recently given a whole new set of products to sell to customers while carrying out my follow up calls. This required constant references to the new information while making customer enquiries. I was able to quickly memorise the key selling points of the products and sold five of them during my first morning sales session.

Criteria: Display an appropriate level of assertiveness when necessary.

Response: In my role as Customer Complaints Officer I am regularly required to display a degree of assertiveness when customers are 'trying it on'. One customer claimed that she had ordered a product which she had not received, although the money had been taken from her account. This wasn't the first time we had experienced this issue with this particular customer. Fortunately, we were in possession of a signed receipt from the Post Office to say the parcel had been delivered. Her husband was the signatory on this occasion. I

was able to provide her with this evidence and she withdrew the complaint after her initial hostility. The situation did not recur.

Criteria: Display skills in basic research and extracting information when relevant to customer needs.

Response: Again, in my role as Customer Complaints Officer I was selling the new products that I was still unfamiliar with to my customers. One asked specific questions about the context of the products and where they were used. This was regarding the function of our kitchen ware at a specific temperature. I was able to quickly extract the information by researching our new website mock-up and provide her with what she needed to know. She was really pleased and ordered two dozen items for her new industrial kitchen.

Criteria: Show a clear focus on and understanding of community needs.

Response: This answer is drawn from experience in my personal life. Our community has been struggling since the threatened closure of a playgroup during school holidays due to budget cuts. My father is a council member and I was able to persuade him to let me arrange a meeting to discuss how we could arrange voluntary supervision of the playgroup among the local parents. During the meeting, the council agreed to partly fund the project on the condition that we would raise the shortfall within the community. My understanding of community needs was a clear benefit to the community in this situation.

Criteria: Demonstrate a clear high level of self-motivation and an ability to work with minimal supervision. This should be evidenced through high levels of productivity.

Response: While working as a Telesales Assistant when I first joined my current employer, my line manager was suddenly off ill and I was left to set my own sales targets (with agreement) broken down into key performance indicators, that is, number of calls made, number of customers spoken to, positive responses, leads and actual orders. Within the two weeks my manager was off sick I managed to exceed all of the key performance indicators and bring in three brand new customers. I received a quarterly bonus on top of our team bonus for my efforts.

Criteria: Demonstrate a positive and flexible attitude and an ability to adapt to changing situations and new working practices.

Response: Last year, our company was bought out by a venture capitalist group to save us from going into administration. My role had some extra responsibilities added to it involving quality assurance which I was not familiar with. With some training I began to understand the requirements and adapted the audit side of the work into each of my customer orders. This was a fluid and constantly changing situation for several weeks with a high degree of uncertainty but I made every effort to ensure both the customers and the new owners were satisfied.

TEN TOP TIPS AND ONE USEFUL ACRONYM FOR COMPLETING THE APPLICATION FORM

- Always write – or type out – a rough draft first using either a photocopy or scanned copy of the application form.

- Check that your handwriting or your typed information is legible, error-free and grammatically correct.

- Avoid jargon wherever you can; keep your language simple and straightforward.

- Read all of the questions carefully – have you actually answered what you are being asked? Read and reread the question. What is it actually asking and have you answered it adequately?

- Read through your CV. Highlight the achievements and positions that demonstrate that you possess transferable skills that are relevant to the role of Fire Control Operator.

- Run your draft application through an online spellchecker to ensure that there are no obvious mistakes. When we've been reading and rereading a piece of writing for what seems like hours we miss the obvious typographical errors. Once you've done that, or if you've handwritten your draft, ask a trusted friend or colleague to read through it for you – preferably one or two trusted friends or colleagues if you can. Ask them to provide you with honest and constructive feedback.

- Review all of your answers. Have you explained what you did, how you did it and what the actual outcome was that is did it make a difference to your company?

- Keep a copy of your own for future reference so you know what you've actually said when it comes to the interview itself.

- Don't provide unnecessary information, you only have a limited space for your answers in most cases. You can safely assume that the person assessing your application will possess a thorough understanding of local procedures.

- Take your time in completing the form. Vacancies for the position of FCOp are not advertised every week; they only arise infrequently and are often oversubscribed with numbers of applicants. Make every effort to maximise your chances.

A useful acronym to remember while completing your application form is ASPIRE:

- **A — Appropriate** — All of your examples should be appropriate to the Fire Control Operator Role.

- **S — Specific** — Avoid generalisations, make your examples specific.

- **P — Positive** — Don't use examples that may raise doubts over your ability to meet the criteria for the job. Focus on your strengths.

- **I — Individual** — Emphasise your achievements, not those that were accomplished by a team that you were a part of.

- **R — Relevant** — Are you answering the question that is actually being asked?

- **E — Emphasise** — Provide clear explanations of the actions you took and why.

Once you have completed the application form, read through it again, bearing in mind the above points. Can you give a resounding positive answer to all of them? If you can't, you will need to review what you have written and focus on the weaker areas you have identified.

Within the next section of the guide I will provide you with some useful test questions to help you prepare for the Fire Control Operator assessment centre.

CHAPTER FOUR

SAMPLE TESTS

Within this section of the guide I will provide you with some useful tests to help you prepare for the Fire Control Operator selection process. It is important to stress from the outset that the tests can vary from Fire Service to Fire Service. This is especially the case for Fire Brigades such as London, simply because the London Fire Brigade privatised the handling of its 999 calls to a third party organisation who will have an entirely different selection procedure to that of a "proper" Fire and Rescue Service.

The selection tests usually consist of the following 3 elements.

Audio Typing: this consists of listening to passages read out by an individual or from an audio recording device played out loud into the room. The aim of this test is to assess your typing speed, spelling, accuracy, listening skills and also your interpretation of what is being said. The content you

provide will be examined and even though you may not finish the passage, as long as the example is accurate and spelling is good this will be considered.

Word Comprehension: this is the ability to read text, process it and understand its meaning. This is tested by reading a passage that will then give a choice of the correct spelling and the meaning of the word. For example: *"The presence of the man in the room"* could also be written as *"The presents of the man in the room."* Both sound the same, but the written context is totally different.

Presence = the fact or condition of being present within your immediate surroundings or vicinity.

Presents = a gift or showing and giving, or an introduction.

Number Recall: this again, is either verbally given from a representative or a recording played in the room. A sequence of numbers is given, initially a lower set of numbers is given, i.e. **2928**. Then, as the test progresses, the length of sequence will increase i.e. **4935742**, and so on. You are required to write down the numbers in the correct sequence on your test paper. This test is used for listening and accuracy skills. Numbers are used to a high percentage of the working day within the role of an Operator and therefore, you need to demonstrate that your memory retention ability is high.

AUDIO TYPING TEST AND THE NUMBER RECALL TEST

I have created an audio typing test and also a number recall test for you at the following website:

www.AudioTypingTest.co.uk

WORD COMPREHENSION TEST 1

During the first word comprehension test you are to circle the correct spelling to match the definition in brackets for questions 1–20.

You have 5 minutes to complete the test.

1. write / right (to express in words)

2. holy / wholly (complete/entirely)

3. conscience / conscious (sense of right and wrong)

4. maze / maize (labyrinth)

5. feint / faint (unclear)

6. fete / fate (outdoor event)

7. repeal / repel (to hold back/regret)

8. rein / reign (to rule)

9. sale / sail (an auction/reduction)

10. cite / site (to quote as authority)

11. queue / cue (to stand in line)

12. quiet / quite (considerably/somewhat)

13. acquire / enquire (to obtain/to get hold of)

14. story / storey (a block in a building)

15. scene / seen (division of a play)

16. teem / team (abundant/overflowing)

17. waive / wave (to forgo/give up the right)

18. stare / stair (to look continuously)

19. tail / tale (a story)

20. wring / ring (to squeeze/twist)

 how2become

ANSWERS TO WORD COMPREHENSION TEST 1

1. write

2. wholly

3. conscious

4. maze

5. feint

6. fete

7. repel

8. reign

9. sale

10. cite

11. queue

12. quite

13. acquire

14. storey

15. scene

16. teem

17. waive

18. stare

19. tale

20. wring

WORD COMPREHENSION TEST 2

You have 10 minutes to complete test 2.

Q1. The pilot . . . . the helicopter back to basecamp due . . . . the strong winds and . . . . down pour.

Which of the following combinations of words is the only one which can be inserted into the sentence?

A. navigates, to, terrential

B. navegates, to, terrential

C. navigator, two, torrential

D. navigated, to, torrential

E. navigated, to, terrential

Answer

Q2. Prior to the airplane taking off, the . . . . informs . . . . about the safety . . . . and key information about flying.

Which of the following combinations of words is the only one which can be inserted into the sentence?

A. stewardess, passengers, procedures

B. steward's, passangers, procedure

C. stewardess, passenger, procedure

D. stewardess, passenger, proseedure

E. Stewardest, passengors, procedure

Answer

Q3. The police . . . . holding a suspect on very little . . . . If they do not find any other proof, they will have to let the suspect go based on law . . . .

Which one the following combinations of words is the only one which can be inserted into the sentence?

A. where, evidence, enforcements

B. were, evidance, inforcements

C. were, evidence, enforcements

D. wear, evidonce, enforcement

E. were, evidence, inforcement

Answer

Q4. The police followed through on a . . . . given by someone who . . . . a drunk man becoming aggressive at a store owner. They decided to send out a patrol car to . . . . and deal with the situation.

Which one the following combinations of words is the only one which can be inserted into the sentence?

A. statement, witnesses, analyze

B. statement, witness, analise

C. statment, witnessed, analyse

D. statement, witnessed, analyse

E. statement, witness', analyze

Answer

Q5. An . . . . was called out to attend to people involved in a car . . . . There were two cars involved and five people were hurt from the . . . .

Which one the following combinations of words is the only one which can be inserted into the sentence?

A. ambulance, colision, aciddent

B. ambulance, collision, accidant

C. ambulance, coalision, accidant

D. ambulence, collision, accident

E. ambulance, collision, accident

Answer

Q6. The shop . . . . was helping a lady pick out an outfit for a wedding. The woman wanted an outfit that was 'classy, ... and . . . .'.

Which one of the following combinations of words is the only one which can be inserted into the sentence?

A. assistant, elegant, feminine

B. asisstant, elegant, feminine

C. assistant, elegent, femininity

D. assistance, ellegent, feminnine

E. assistent, elegant, feminine

Answer

Q7. A postgraduate student decided to go . . . . for a year before getting a job. He wanted to . . . . different cultures, ... and ways of living.

Which one of the following combinations of words is the only one which can be inserted into the sentence?

A. travel, experience, lifestyles

B. travelling, experience, lifestyles

C. travels, experiance, lifestyles

D. travelling, experiance, lifestyles

E. travelling, experience, life style

Answer

Q8. A school trip has been . . . . for pupils to go to Dover Castle. Teachers . . . . not only will it be an experience for the students, but will also help with their . . . .

Which one of the following combinations of words is the only one which can be inserted into the sentence?

A. arrange, believe, education

B. aranged, beleive, education

C. arranged, believe, education

D. arranged, beleive, educashion

E. arange, believe, edducation

Answer

Q9. Each . . . . firefighter has be at the station within 5 minutes of being called on a . . . . pager. This provides a quick and . . . . service.

Which one of the following combinations of words is the only one which can be inserted into the sentence?

A. retained, personel, efficiant

B. rettained, personel, efficient

C. retain, personal, eficient

D. retained, personal, efficient

E. retained, personal, effiant

Answer

Q10. The . . . . government had to change its . . . . and send another . . . . to the Supreme Court.

Which one of the following combinations of words is the only one which can be inserted into the sentence?

A. federal, aproch, propozition

B. federel, approach, proppostion

C. federal, approch, proposishion

D. federel, aproach, proposition

E. federal, approach, proposition

Answer

ANSWERS TO WORD COMPREHENSION TEST 2

Q1. D

Q2. A

Q3. C

Q4. D

Q5. E

Q6. A

Q7. B

Q8. C

Q9. D

Q10. E

WORD COMPREHENSION TEST 3

You have 10 minutes to complete the test.

Q1. Which one of the following sentences is grammatically correct?

A.   I wishes you the very best of luck.

B.   Our holiday as been postponed.

C.   The Government is implementing a new law today.

D.   It is difficult to understood my teacher.

Answer

Q2. Which one of the following sentences is grammatically correct?

A.   Please right your name and address on the letter provided

B.   Every day he bring me flowers

C.   Our teacher was of sick today

D.   We are pleased to inform you that you have won a prize

Answer

Q3. Which one of the following sentences is grammatically correct?

A. We will be in contact with you shortly.

B. We regret to be in contact with you shortly.

C. Shortly, we will be in contract with you.

D. We will be in contact with you shortley.

Answer

Q4. Which one of the following sentences is grammatically correct?

A. The queen is bout to give a speech.

B. I get really nervous when I am about to give a speech.

C. Giving speech makes me really nervous.

D. Speaking in front of people makes me nerves.

Answer

Q5. Which one of the following is grammatically correct?

A. Yours sincerity.

B. Your's sincerely.

C. Yours sincerely.

D. You're sincerely.

Answer

Q6. Which one of the following sentences is grammatically correct?

A. The president gives speech on national television.

B. We are pleased to inform you that your flight is delayed.

C. We regret to inform you that you have won a holiday.

D. We agree to the terms and conditions.

Answer

Q7. Which one of the following sentences is grammatically correct?

A. Noone likes to be left alone.

B. The lawyer bespoke upon her behalf.

C. The police arrested a man for criminal damage.

D. The train line informed that the train would be delayed.

Answer

Q8. Which one of the following sentences is grammatically correct?

A. The director stopped filming because the actors messed up their lines.

B. The producer were happy for finishing the filming.

C. The acters were doing the best they can.

D. Filming onset can be nervous experience.

Answer

Q9. Which one of the following sentences is grammatically correct?

A. The police has new suspect.

B. The police have a new suspect.

C. The police as a new lead.

D. The police not have any leads to go on.

Answer

Q10. Which one of the following sentences is grammatically correct?

A. We our pleased to inform you that your application was successful.

B. We regret to inform you that you're application was successful.

C. The firefighter service is more than just putting out fires.

D. The ambulance service is important role within the medical profession.

Answer

Now check your answers carefully before moving onto the next test.

ANSWERS TO WORD COMPREHENSION TEST 3

Q1. C

Q2. D

Q3. A

Q4. B

Q5. C

Q6. D

Q7. C

Q8. A

Q9. B

Q10. C

Now move onto the next test.

WORD COMPREHENSION TEST 4

You have 15 minutes to complete this test.

Q1. Which two words are most opposite in meaning?

Embellished, exaggerated, reduced, standard, overstated, elaborate

Answer

Q2. Which two words are most opposite in meaning?

Frightened, panicked, worried, ecstatic, worried, overrated

Answer

Q3. Which two words are most opposite in meaning?

Peaceful, calm, tranquil, indulge, divert, idyllic

Answer

Q4. Which two words are most opposite in meaning?

Important, famished, significant, noteworthy, momentous, calm

Answer

Q5. Which two words are most opposite in meaning?

Friendly, sociable, welcoming, ignorant, competent, pleasant

Answer

Q6. Which two words are most opposite in meaning?

Imaginary, fictional, unreal, legible, vague

Answer

Q7. Which two words are most opposite in meaning?

Treason, biased, betrayal, disloyalty, honest, sedition

Answer

Q8. Which two words are most opposite in meaning?

Vigorous, exhausted, fatigued, feeble, weary, drained

Answer

Q9. Which two words are most opposite in meaning?

Hatred, sympathy, loathe, callous, animosity, hostility

Answer

Q10. Which two words are most opposite in meaning?

Condemn, affection, love, praise, adore, admire

Answer

Q11. Which two words are most opposite in meaning?

Conclusion, decision, outcome, initiation, result, probability

Answer

Q12. Which two words are most opposite in meaning?

Playful, subdued, submissive, quiet, lethargic, lament

Answer

Q13. Which two words are most opposite in meaning?

Imaginary, realistic, illegible, impracticable, radical, embellished

Answer

Q14. Which two words are most opposite in meaning?

Fantasy, unfeasible, pretend, imagined, reality, fiction

Answer

Q15. Which two words are most opposite in meaning?

Fabrication, misrepresentation, construction, inaccurate, distortion, authenticity

Answer

Now check your answers carefully before moving onto the next test.

ANSWERS TO WORD COMPREHENSION TEST 4

Q1. Reduced and standard

Q2. Ecstatic and overrated

Q3. Indulge and divert

Q4. Famished and calm

Q5. Ignorant and competent

Q6. Legible and vague

Q7. Honest and biased

Q8. Vigorous and feeble

Q9. Sympathy and callous

Q10. Condemn and praise

Q11. Initiation and probability

Q12. Playful and lament

Q13. Realistic and impracticable

Q14. Unfeasible and reality

Q15. Inaccurate and authenticity

Now move onto to the next sample test.

WORD COMPREHENSION TEST 5

You have 15 minutes to complete this test.

Q1. In the following question you are given two definitions and two words. Place the correct word by each definition.

Noun: the feeling that something is real or true

. . . .

Adjective: that can be accepted as true

. . . .

believable, belief

Q2. In the following question you are given two definitions and two words. Place the correct word by each definition.

Noun: people who gives disapproval

. . . .

Adjective: looking for faults or problems

. . . .

criticism, critical

Q3. In the following question you are given two definitions and two words. Place the correct word by each definition.

Noun: to settle an argument/ to choose/ to make up one's mind

. . . .

Adjective: clear, definite

. . . .

decision, decided

Q4. In the following question you are given two definitions and two words. Place the correct word by each definition.

Noun: argument

. . . .

Adjective: something that can be questioned or argued about

. . . .

disputable, dispute

Q5. In the following question you are given two definitions and two words. Place the correct word by each definition.

Noun: a noise, sight, sound preventing concentration

. . . .

Adjective: unable to concentrate properly

. . . .

distraction, distracted

Q6. In the following question you are given two definitions and two words. Place the correct word by each definition.

Noun: personal respect

. . . .

Adjective: ethical, fair, moral, principled

. . . .

honourable, honour

Q7. In the following question you are given two definitions and two words. Place the correct word by each definition.

Noun: the ability to create images that are not present

. . . .

Adjective: existing only in the mind

. . . .

imagination, imaginary

Q8. In the following question you are given two definitions and two words. Place the correct word by each definition.

Noun: annoyance, slight pain

. . . .

Adjective: easily annoyed

. . . .

irritable, irritation

Q9. In the following question you are given two definitions and two words. Place the correct word by each definition.

Noun: probability

. . . .

Adjective: probably

. . . .

likelihood, likely

Q10. In the following question you are given two definitions and two words. Place the correct word by each definition.

Noun: art or philosophy of reasoning

. . . .

Adjective: clear, rational, reasonable

. . . .

logic, logical

Q11. In the following question you are given two definitions and two words. Place the correct word by each definition.

Noun: a sign, advertisement or warning

. . . .

Adjective: attracting attention, easily seen

. . . .

notice, noticeable

Q12. In the following question you are given two definitions and two words. Place the correct word by each definition.

Noun: act, play, achievement

. . . .

Adjective: doing or acting

. . . .

performing, performance

Q13. In the following question you are given two definitions and two words. Place the correct word by each definition.

Noun: defence / safety

. . . .

Adjective: trying or intended to protect

. . . .

protection, protective

Q14. In the following question you are given two definitions and two words. Place the correct word by each definition.

Noun: worthy of respect

. . . .

Adjective: showing consideration or politeness

. . . .

respectful, respectability

Q15. In the following question you are given two definitions and two words. Place the correct word by each definition.

Noun: pleasure, pride, sense of fulfilment

. . . .

Adjective: acceptable, fair, good enough

. . . .

satisfactory, satisfaction

Now check your answers carefully before moving onto the next test.

ANSWERS TO WORD COMPREHENSION TEST 5

Q1. Noun – belief, Adjective – believable

Q2. Noun – criticism, Adjective – critical

Q3. Noun – decision, Adjective – decided

Q4. Noun – dispute, Adjective – disputable

Q5. Noun – distraction, Adjective – distracted

Q6. Noun – honour, Adjective – honourable

Q7. Noun – imagination, Adjective – imaginary

Q8. Noun – irritation, Adjective – irritable

Q9. Noun – likelihood, Adjective – likely

Q10. Noun – logic, Adjective – logical

Q11. Noun – notice, Adjective – noticeable

Q12. Noun – performance, Adjective – performing

Q13. Noun – protection, Adjective – protective

Q14. Noun – respectability, Adjective – respectful

Q15. Noun – satisfaction, Adjective – satisfactory

Now move onto the next test.

JUMBLED UP SENTENCES

Within each question you will see a jumbled up sentence. Put the brackets containing parts of the sentence in the best order for the whole sentence to make sense. You are given the first two words of each sentence. Before you attempt the test, take a look at the following sample questions:

Sample test question 1

Carol expects (to make her) (me) (a party dress)

Answer: Carol expects me to make her a party dress.

Sample test question 2

What did (do) (out) (?) (with those) (had) (old) (thrown) (clothes I) (you)

Answer: What did you do with those old clothes I had thrown out?

Once you understand the test, move on to JUMBLED UP SENTENCES TEST 1 which consist of 25 sample questions. You have 15 minutes to complete the test.

JUMBLED UP SENTENCES EXERCISE 1

Within each question you will see a jumbled up sentence. Put the brackets containing parts of the sentence in the best order for the whole sentence to make sense. You are given the first two words of each sentence.

Q1. Carol expects (to make her) (me) (a party dress)

Q2. It would (bitter fruit) (that) (foolish to) (eat) (be)

Q3. My mum (her) and (friend) wanted (go) to a party (out)

Q4. It would be (if she did not) a problem (do her homework)

Q5. My brother (I) and went out (the) to park (a) on sunny day

Q6. It would (Important) be (her) moment in academic (an) career

Q7. It would (a good idea) be (before going out to play) to finish your homework

Q8. James likes (at night) (his dog) (to walk)

Q9. Reading Sheet (is) music (tricky) (sometimes)

Q10. Sarah is (to) keen (try) (team) (out) (for the)

Q11. Some (Dinosaurs) (were) (than a) (two) (house) (taller) (Storey)

Q12. John wanted (down the park) (to take the dog) (out for a walk)

Q13. Bella had (that she) (her work) (for) (was being assessed) (no idea)

Q14. James went (watch a) (to) (to Wembley Stadium) (football match)

Q15. The dog (chase the postman) (had) (from the house) (to) (escaped)

Q16. The shopping (holiday) (for) (had closed) (centre) (bank)

Q17. Mia was (to) asked (the) (join) dance academy

Q18. My best (I) friend and (shopping) went for (mum's) my birthday

```
┌────────────────────────────────────────────────────┐
│                                                    │
│                                                    │
│                                                    │
└────────────────────────────────────────────────────┘
```

Q19. I had (for) to write 8,000 words (my) for dissertation. (Was) it a relief (it was) when finished

```
┌────────────────────────────────────────────────────┐
│                                                    │
│                                                    │
│                                                    │
└────────────────────────────────────────────────────┘
```

Q20. My (I) mum me (tells) sing (cannot)

```
┌────────────────────────────────────────────────────┐
│                                                    │
│                                                    │
│                                                    │
└────────────────────────────────────────────────────┘
```

Q21. I went (fishing) on a (trip) my with (brother)

```
┌────────────────────────────────────────────────────┐
│                                                    │
│                                                    │
│                                                    │
└────────────────────────────────────────────────────┘
```

Q22. I started (job) my (today) new. (Was) I extremely nervous

```
┌────────────────────────────────────────────────────┐
│                                                    │
│                                                    │
│                                                    │
└────────────────────────────────────────────────────┘
```

Q23. I like (read) to and (mystery) suspense books, (are) they exciting

```
┌────────────────────────────────────────────────────┐
│                                                    │
│                                                    │
│                                                    │
└────────────────────────────────────────────────────┘
```

Q24. I was (by) overwhelmed (thought)

```



```

Q25. For lunch (for) I had a (sandwich) ham (cup) and a of tea

```



```

Now check your answers carefully.

ANSWERS TO JUMBLED UP SENTENCES EXERCISE 1

Q1.   Carol expects me to make her a party dress.

Q2.   It would be foolish to eat that bitter fruit.

Q3.   My mum and her friend wanted to go out to a party.

Q4.   It would be a problem if she did not do her homework.

Q5.   My brother and I went out to the park on a sunny day.

Q6.   It would be an important moment in her academic career.

Q7.   It would be a good idea to finish your homework before going out to play.

Q8.   James likes to walk his dog at night.

Q9.   Reading Sheet music is sometimes tricky.

Q10. Sarah is keen to try out for the team.

Q11. Some Dinosaurs were taller than a two storey house.

Q12. John wanted to take the dog out for a walk down the park.

Q13. Bella had no idea that she was being assessed for her work.

Q14. James went to Wembley Stadium to watch a football match.

Q15. The dog escaped from the house to chase the postman.

Q16. The shopping centre had closed for bank holiday.

Q17. Mia was asked to join the dance academy.

Q18. My best friend and I went shopping for my mum's birthday

Q19. I had to write 8,000 words for my dissertation. It was a relief when it was finished.

Q20. My mum tells me I cannot sing

Q21. I went on a fishing trip with my brother

Q22. I started my new job today. I was extremely nervous.

Q23. I like to read mystery and suspense books, they are exciting.

Q24. I was overwhelmed by thought

Q25. For lunch I had a ham sandwich and a cup of tea

Once you have checked your answers please move onto exercise 2.

JUMBLED UP SENTENCES EXERCISE 2

Within each question you will see a jumbled up sentence. Put the brackets containing parts of the sentence in the best order for the whole sentence to make sense. You are given the first two words of each sentence. You have 15 minutes to complete the test.

Q26. My boyfriend (and) celebrated (I) (one) our year anniversary

Q27. My favourite (is) film Saving Private Ryan because the (of) emotion and (line) story behind it

Q28. My happiest memory (a) is day (snowy)

Q29. My best (party) birthday (when) was (I) 12. (Went) we ice skating (London) in

Q30. My favourite (of) type (is) dancing Latin and Ballroom

Q31. I like (watch) to the (leaves) the falling (the) in autumn

Q32. I like (drink) to (coffees) cappuccino and (biscuits) eat

Q33. It was (hot) a (sunny) and day, (I) so decided to (feed) and (go) the ducks

Q34. I received (not) detention for (attention) paying

Q35. I like (go) to (in) singing (rain) the

Q36. Everyone is (on) going holiday (the) for summer

Q37. My mum (dad) and have decided (take) to us fishing

 how2become

Q38. Camping is (a) way (great) to escape (some) for (and) peace quiet

Q39. All you (is) can do (best) your

Q40. The truth (absolute) is

Q41. A man's friend (best) (his) is dog

Q42. No one (left) behind) gets or forgotten

Q43. Somebody told (this) me that is the (where) place everything (better) is and (safe) is everything

Q44. It is (things) funny how (out) turn

Q45. Life is (make) it what you

Q46. On a (day) rainy, (sit) I in doors (have) and a duvet day

Q47. I still (fairy) believe in tales

Q48. Social media has (an) become (sensation) internet

Q49. Mr brother (I) and best (are) friends first, brother sister (and) second

Q50. On the weekends like (I) hanging out (my) with family and (films) watch

Now check your answers carefully.

ANSWERS TO JUMBLED UP SENTENCES EXERCISE 2

Q26. My boyfriend and I celebrated our one year anniversary.

Q27. My favourite film is Saving Private Ryan because of the emotion and story line behind it.

Q28. My happiest memory is a snowy day.

Q29. My best birthday party was when I was 12. We went ice skating in London.

Q30. My favourite type of dancing is Latin and Ballroom.

Q31. I like to watch the leaves falling in the autumn.

Q32. I like to drink cappuccino coffees and eat biscuits.

Q33. It was a hot and sunny day, so I decided to go and feed the ducks.

Q34. I received detention for not paying attention.

Q35. I like to go singing in the rain.

Q36. Everyone is going on holiday for the summer.

Q37. My mum and dad have decided to take us fishing.

Q38. Camping is a great way to escape for some peace and quiet.

Q39. All you can do is your best.

Q40. The truth is absolute.

Q41. A man's best friend is his dog.

Q42. No one gets left behind or forgotten.

Q43. Somebody told me that this is the place where everything is better and everything is safe.

Q44. It is funny how things turn out.

Q45. Life is what you make it.

Q46. On a rainy day, I sit in doors and have a duvet day.

Q47. I still believe in fairy tales.

Q48. Social media has become an internet sensation.

Q49. My brother and I are best friends first, brother and sister second.

Q50. On the weekends I like to hang out with my family and watch films.

Now move onto the next test.

SENTENCES WITH MISSING WORDS

In this type of test question you will see sentences each with a missing word. You have a choice of 4 words with which to fill the gap in each sentence. Select the word which best completes each sentence. Give one answer for each question. Study the example before you begin the four exercises to make sure you understand how to do the test.

Sample question 1

Is this the place . . . . you saw the accident?

1. which

2. when

3. where

4. who

ANSWER: where

Sample question 2

The thief escaped . . . . the open gate.

1. under

2. through

3. over

4. on

Answer: through

Once you understand the sample questions move onto the exercises that follow.

SENTENCES WITH MISSING WORDS EXERCISE 1

There are 25 questions and you have 12 minutes to complete the test.

Q1. She was told to lock the dog up to stop the danger . . . . again.

1. occuring

2. ocurring

3. occurring

4. ocuring

Answer

Q2. The finder was advised to take the umbrella to the lost . . . . office.

1. propperty

2. proparty

3. property

4. properrty

Answer

Q3. Richard spent literally hours working on the . . . . of work.

1. peace

2. peice

3. pease

4. pees

Answer

Q4. Sarah had to deal with an angry customer, but she did not deal with them . . . .

1. properlly

2. properly

3. properley

4. properrly

Answer

Q5. She was asked to complete the job in the . . . . manner.

1. ussual

2. usule

3. usuall

4. usual

Answer

Q6. Sarah had no idea . . . . she was going.

1. were

2. where

3. weir

4. wear

Answer

Q7. Sarah was the manager of a company and had to . . . . all the problems.

1. encounter

2. incounter

3. incountar

4. encountar

Answer

Q8. Sarah went to the shops . . . . she was hungry.

1. because

2. becauz

3. becauze

4. beecause

Answer

Q9. Charlotte thought the room looked very . . . .

1. decodent

2. decadent

3. decodence

4. decadence

Answer

Q10. Sarah thinks she may need to go and see an

. . . .

1. opticion

2. optician

3. opticien

4. optishion

Answer

Q11. The teacher tried to give the students good

. . . .

1. example

2. exemple

3. examples

4. exemples

Answer

Q12. For a musician you need to have . . . .

1. creative

2. cretivity

3. creativity

4. creativety

Answer

Q13. In the factory, workers needed to use their

. . . .

1. initiative

2. initative

3. enitiative

4. initiatives

Answer

Q14. The door to the cabin was left . . . .

1. unnlocked

2. unlocked

3. unllocked

4. unloked

Answer

Q15. The argument put forward by Rita had no
. . . . to the case.

1. significanse

2. significans

3. significance

4. significunce

Answer

Q16. The . . . . were extending the house.

1. builders

2. bilders

3. billders

4. buillders

Answer

Q17. The students were asked to put forward a
. . . . towards the research.

1. propposition

2. proposition

3. proposishun

4. proposishan

Answer

Q18. The glass lens in the . . . . had smashed.

1. specticles

2. speticuls

3. specticals

4. spectacles

Answer

Q19. On a field trip, the students were asked to . . . .
the natural environment.

1. obsserv

2. observe

3. observation

4. obsurve

Answer

Q20. The twins wanted to go for a walk but it was . . . .
wet.

1. two

2. too

3. to

4. tooh

Answer

Q21. The doctors said that the man was in a critical but . . . . condition.

1. staple

2. stable

3. stayble

4. staball

Answer

Q22. Sending flowers to a funeral is a . . . . gesture.

1. foughtful

2. thoughtful

3. faughtful

4. thortfall

Answer

Q23. Geography students are taught how to look after the . . . .

1. invironment

2. envirament

3. environment

4. invirenment

Answer

Q24. One of the students in the class always seemed to be a

. . . .

1. probalem

2. problem

3. problam

4. probelem

Answer

Q25. Steve and Michael . . . . in a battle of thumb wars.

1. thought

2. fought

3. thwart

4. fault

Answer

Now check your answers before moving on to the next exercise.

ANSWERS TO SENTENCES WITH MISSING WORDS EXERCISE 1

Q1. occurring

Q2. property

Q3. peice

Q4. properly

Q5. usual

Q6. where

Q7. encounter

Q8. because

Q9. decadent

Q10. optician

Q11. examples

Q12. creativity

Q13. initiative

Q14. unlocked

Q15. significance

Q16. builders

Q17. proposition

Q18. spectacles

Q19. observe

Q20. too

Q21. stable

Q22. thoughtful

Q23. environment

Q24. problem

Q25. fought

Now move on to the next exercise.

SENTENCES WITH MISSING WORDS EXERCISE 2

There are 25 questions and you have 12 minutes to complete the test.

Q26. The teacher told the child that his behaviour was not
. . . .

1. exceptable

2. acceptable

3. acceptible

4. exceptible

Answer

Q27. The child was trying to . . . . some knowledge for her class tomorrow.

1. equire

2. acquire

3. acwiar

4. acwire

Answer

Q28. Sarah and Mia got in an . . . . over the same boy.

1. argument

2. arguement

3. argumant

4. areguement

Answer

Q29. Sarah's birthday falls in the last . . . . month.

1. calander

2. calendar

3. kalender

4. calindar

Answer

Q30. It was a . . . . sunny day.

1. bewtiful

2. beutiful

3. beautiful

4. bueteful

Answer

Q31. The neighbour next door was a . . . . man.

1. pompers

2. pompous

3. pomperse

4. pompouse

Answer

Q32. Scientist discovered a new cure which is proving . . . .

1. fenomenal

2. phenomanall

3. phenomenal

4. fennomanal

Answer

Q33. My family went to visit the . . . .

1. Missisippi

2. Mississippi

3. Misisipi

4. Misissippi

Answer

Q34. We went to a jumble sale and found some great

. . . .

1. bargens

2. bargins

3. bargains

4. barggains

Answer

Q35. The work required . . . . skills.

1. pacific

2. spacific

3. specific

4. spesific

Answer

Q36. The job looked promising but it was not . . . .

1. definate

2. deafinite

3. deffinite

4. definite

Answer

Q37. Having a zero-hour contract does not . . . . you any hours.

1. garante

2. garuntee

3. guarantee

4. guarantey

Answer

Q38. The job required needed someone to start

. . . .

1. imideatley

2. emmediatley

3. immediately

4. immeadiatley

Answer

Q39. Please answer the questions using your

. . . .

1. intelligence

2. intellegence

3. inteligence

4. intellegenc

Answer

Q40. Her favourite . . . . activity was skiing.

1.   leshure

2.   lesuir

3.   lesuire

4.   leisure

Answer

Q41. You need a . . . . to drive a car.

1.   lisance

2.   liceance

3.   license

4.   lisence

Answer

Q42. John went to the . . . . to research his paper.

1.   liberary

2.   library

3.   librarey

4.   lybrarey

Answer

Q43. Sarah had a tricky . . . . to do on her driving test.

1.   manoovar

2.   maneouver

3.   maneuver

4.   manoeuvre

Answer

Q44. We . . . . go on holiday.

1.   ocasionaly

2.   occasionally

3.   ocassionally

4.   ocassionally

Answer

Q45. My teacher asked us to write a . . . .

1.   playright

2.   playwrite

3.   playwright

4.   playrite

Answer

Q46. Holly's grandmother had some personal
. . . .

1. poseshions

2. posessions

3. possessions

4. posessions

Answer

Q.47. Sarah knew that the snake was . . . .

1. poissonous

2. poisionous

3. poisonous

4. posinous

Answer

Q48. Sarah's lips were . . . .

1. tremballing

2. trembling

3. trembaling

4. trembleing

Answer

Q49. That book was a work of . . . .

1. ficshon

2. ficshion

3. fiction

4. ficttion

Answer

Q50. That actress received a great deal of . . . .

1. publicity

2. publicaty

3. publisaty

4. publicate

Answer

Now check your answers before moving on to the next exercise.

ANSWERS TO SENTENCES WITH MISSING WORDS EXERCISE 2

Q26. acceptable

Q27. acquire

Q28. argument

Q29. Calendar

Q30. beautiful

Q31. pompous

Q32. phenomenal

Q33. Mississippi

Q34. bargains

Q35. specific

Q36. definite

Q37. guarantee

Q38. immediately

Q39. intelligence

Q40. leisure

Q41. license

Q42. library

Q43. manoeuvre

Q44. occasionally

Q45. playwright

Q46. possessions

Q47. poisonous

Q48. trembling

Q49. fiction

Q50. publicity

Now move on to the interview section of the guide.

CHAPTER FIVE

THE INTERVIEW

During the Fire Control Operator interview you will get asked a series of questions that will assess your suitability for the post. In this section of the guide I will provide you with a number of sample interview questions and responses that will help you to prepare. It is important to note that you MUST provide EVIDENCE of where you meet the assessable competencies that form part of the job description. This can be achieved by responding to the situational interview questions using the STAR method.

S – Situation. This is the specific context to provide you with the information. Try and be as detailed as you can without using the names of people or client companies.

T – Task. This is the actual detail of the issue you were facing and who you had to work with to achieve the outcome of the problem or issue.

A – Action. The action is what it suggests; what you actually did to resolve the situation you were facing. Provide as much information as you can about your personal behaviour within this context. Always focus on the use of 'I', rather than 'We', unless you are being asked to provide examples of working within a team.

R – Results. What was the outcome of your action and how did it affect those around you, whether they were customers or colleagues?

Now let's take a look at a number of sample interview questions and responses. Please note: the following interview questions are not guaranteed to be the ones you will get asked during the interview; however, they are useful guide for helping you to prepare.

SAMPLE QUESTION NUMBER 1

Tell us why you want to become a Fire Control Operator?

Sample response

"I have worked in my current role now for a number of years. I have an excellent employer and enjoy working for them but unfortunately no longer find my job challenging. I understand that the role of a Fire Control Operator is both demanding and rewarding and I believe I have the qualities to thrive in such an environment. I love working under pressure, working as part of a team that is diverse in nature and helping people in difficult situations. The public expectations of the Fire Service are very high and I believe I have the right qualities to help the organisation deliver the right service to the community by becoming a highly competent Fire Control Operator.

I have studied the qualities and competencies required for the role and believe that I have the skills to match them and deliver what they require. I am also looking for a career where the hours are varied. I am not really suited to a normal 9-5 job and I like working shift work. This also very much suits my personal life as I am currently single and have no commitments.

Finally, I want to work in a job that makes a difference to the community in which I live. I have had some experience of working in the community through some voluntary work I carried out earlier this year and I want to carry on working within the community."

Top tips

- Don't be negative about your current or previous employer.
- Be positive, enthusiastic and upbeat in your response.
- Make reference to the qualities and competencies during your response.

SAMPLE QUESTION NUMBER 2

Why have you chosen this particular Fire Service?

Sample response

"I have carried out extensive research into the Fire Service and in particular this one. I have been impressed by the level of service it provides the public and how it always strives to reduce fires and incidents through its proactive community safety work. The website provides the community with direct access to a different range of topics and the work that is being carried out through your Home Fire Safety Risk Assessment teams is impressive. I have looked at the national and local statistics for fire and fire-related incidents and also read many different newspapers and articles about the good work being done by the Fire Service in the county. I like this Fire Service because of its reputation and the people that I have spoken to who work within the Service have told me that they get a great deal of job satisfaction from working here. Finally, because I actually live within the county, I have built up a good level of topographical knowledge which I feel will be an asset to the team."

Top tips

- Research the Fire Service you are applying to join thoroughly and make reference to particular success stories that they have achieved.

- Be positive, enthusiastic and upbeat in your response.

- Be positive about their Fire and Rescue Service and don't be critical of it, even if you think it needs improving in certain areas.

- Finally, if you make reference to fire statistics within your response be prepared to back it up with actual facts and figures.

SAMPLE QUESTION NUMBER 3

What does the role of a Fire Control Operator involve?

Sample response

"Fire Control Operators are the first point of contact for members of the public requesting Fire Service assistance. It is a highly responsible job and one that requires a calm and reassuring nature.

They answer emergency 999 calls and high priority calls as efficiently as possible, obtaining and recording accurate information, assessing the level of Fire Service response required and initiating the appropriate action as quickly as possible.

Where no Fire and Rescue Service action is required, they provide advice and guidance to the caller. In all cases, callers are dealt with in a calm, courteous and professional manner, and if necessary, firmly and assertively to obtain essential information."

Top tips

- Understand the qualities and competencies and be able to recite them word for word when responding to this question.

- Try to speak to current serving Fire Control Operator's in order to try and find out more about the job that they do. You can do this by trying to arrange a familiarisation visit at the Fire Service Control Centre prior to your interview.

- The website of the Fire Service you are applying to join should have information relating to the role of a Fire Control Operator. Learn this information prior to interview.

 how2become

SAMPLE QUESTION NUMBER 4

Have you ever lost your temper?

This is a great interview question and is not easy to answer. All of us have lost our temper at some point, but you need to be careful as to how much you disclose. Part of the role of a Fire Control Operator is to remain calm under pressure and you need to demonstrate this in your response. They do not want to employ people who lose their temper when dealing with 999 calls. It is during these times that you will need to use your skills to calm people down and also have the ability to filter out hoax calls.

The question is designed to see how honest you are, and whether you are a naturally aggressive person. It is ok to lose your temper at times during your personal life, but it is not welcome as a Fire Control Operator.

Sample response

"In the whole I am a calm person and do not become aggressive or confrontational.

Whilst it is only natural to be annoyed with people from time to time, I see no point in losing my temper. It is just wasted energy. I understand that Fire Control Operators cannot lose their temper with callers as it would be highly unprofessional and deter from the reason why they are there; to extract the information required in order to dispatch the appropriate response in the fastest time possible. I appreciate that it must be frustrating at times dealing with hoax callers, but the way to resolve issues is to remain calm and be patient."

Key areas to consider:

- Try to use 'non-confrontational' words and phrases during your response – patience, calm, understanding, etc.

- Demonstrate your understanding of the role and the importance of remaining calm and professional.

SAMPLE QUESTION NUMBER 5

How do you feel about working with people from different cultures and backgrounds?

This is quite a common interview question and one that you need to be prepared for. Respect for diversity is essential to the role of a Fire Control Operator as you will be dealing with and working with people from different cultures and backgrounds. We live in a diverse community that brings many positive aspects that we can learn from. When answering the question, you should be aiming to demonstrate that you are totally at ease when working with people from different cultures and backgrounds. You may wish to give an example of this in your response. Take a look at the following response to this question. Remember to be honest in your reply and only state the facts about your feelings towards people from different cultures. If you are not truthful in your response, you will not be doing yourself, or the Fire Service, any favours.

Sample response

"I am totally at ease in those situations, in fact I don't even think about it. This has never been a problem for me. I have a sincere interest in people from different cultures and backgrounds and have learnt many things from them in the past. I would like to think that we can all learn something from everybody, regardless of their culture or background and this is a part of the job that I would look forward to.

There are so many different and exciting things to learn in life and this can only be achieved by meeting, respecting and understanding people from different cultures and backgrounds. Teams that are diverse in nature have a better chance of delivering a higher quality of service. If the community in which the police force serves is diverse, then so should the workforce that delivers the service.

With regards to the role of a Fire Control Operator, I would very much look forward to working with and interacting with people from different cultures and backgrounds. I also feel it is very important for the Fire Service team to represent the community in which it serves. This will assist the Fire Service in building trust and confidence within the community and also help the organisation to achieve its aim of reducing fires and fire-related incidents."

Key areas to consider:

- Be honest when answering this type of question.

- Demonstrate that you understand diversity and the benefits this brings to society. Provide examples where appropriate.

SAMPLE QUESTION NUMBER 6

If you witnessed a member of your team being bullied or harassed at work what action would you take and why?

There is only one answer to this question and that is that you would take action to stop it, providing it was safe to do so. Bullying or harassment of any kind must not be tolerated. The second part of the question is just as important. They are asking you why you would take this particular action.

Before you prepare your answer to this question think carefully about what action you would take if somebody was being bullied or harassed. Taking action can mean a number of different things ranging from reporting the incident to your manager, through to intervention.

Whatever answer you give it is important that you are honest and tell the truth about how you would respond to such a situation. Take a look at the following sample response to this question.

Sample response

"I would stop it immediately if it was safe to do so. This type of behaviour is totally unacceptable and must not be tolerated in the workplace. The reason why I would take action is because if I didn't, then I would effectively be condoning the bullying or harassment. The type of action I would take would very much depend on the circumstances. In most cases I would intervene at the time of the incident and ask the person to stop the bullying or harassment.

If the incident were very serious, then I would report it to my line manager at the Fire Control Centre so that further action could be taken. Whatever the situation was, I would definitely take steps to stop it from happening. I believe that I would also have a duty under Fire Service policy to take action to stop bullying and harassment."

SAMPLE QUESTION 7

What do you understand about the term equality and fairness?

Treating everybody with respect and dignity is important in everyday life. Treat others how you would expect to be treated regardless of their age, gender, sexual orientation or cultural background.

If you are not capable of treating people with respect and dignity then the Fire Service is not for you!

A question based on this subject is likely to come up during the interview and it relates to the quality of being able to work with others.

The following is a sample response to this question.

Sample response
"Equality and fairness is about treating people with dignity and respect and without discrimination. Unfair discrimination in employment is wrong. It is bad for the individuals who are denied jobs or who suffer victimisation or harassment because of prejudice. I understand that within the Fire and Rescue Service it is the responsibility of everyone to uphold the principles and policies of the organisation in relation to equality and fairness. Discrimination or unacceptable behaviour of any sort is not tolerated and nor should it be. Not only is it important to apply these principles whilst working with colleagues in the Fire Service but it also applies when serving the public."

SAMPLE QUESTION 8

Do you have any experience of working as a team member?

The ability to work effectively in a team is an extremely important aspect of the role. Not only will you be spending a great deal of time together at work, you will also depend on your colleagues during stressful incidents in the control room. Therefore it is important that you can demonstrate you have the ability to work as an effective team member. You must also be capable of working as part of a wider team with the other emergency services, stakeholders and key parties.

When responding to this type of question, try to think of occasions when you have been part of a team and achieved a common goal.

Maybe you are already involved in team sports playing hockey, rugby or football? You may also find that you have experience of working as a team member through work. If you have no or very little experience of working as a team member then try to get some before you apply to the Fire Service as a Fire Control Operator. After all, teamwork is an important aspect of the role.

Now take a look at the following sample response.

Sample response

"Yes, I have many years' experience of working in a team environment. To begin with, I have been playing hockey for my local team for the last three years. We worked really hard together improving our skills over the course of last season and we managed to win the league.

I am also very much involved in teamwork in my current job. I work as a nurse at the local hospital and in order for the ward

to function correctly we must work effectively as a team. My job is to check all of the patients at the beginning of my shift and also make sure that we have enough medical supplies to last the duration. It is then my responsibility to inform the ward sister that the checks have been carried out. She will then obtain more supplies if we need them.

We have to work very closely together for many hours and we all pull together whenever the going gets tough. I enjoy working in a team environment and feel comfortable whilst working under pressure.

The key qualities and attributes required to work effectively as a team member are communication, both listening and verbally, supporting other team members when required, ensuring the team follows a specific brief, team members following their training and guidelines and also being able to adapt to a constant changing environment. It is also important for the team to review and reflect upon their performance following every task so that they can improve for the next time."

SAMPLE QUESTION 9

If a member of the public asked you how to call the Fire Service if they had an emergency, what advice would you give them?

This question is not a common one but there have been occasions when it has been asked during the interview. If you are going to be a Fire Control Operator then you certainly should know how to call the Fire Service in the event of an emergency.

The answer is a simple one and the following is a sample response to help you.

Sample response

"I would tell them to dial 999 using the nearest available working phone.

I'd also inform them that they can use their mobile phone to dial 999 even if they do not have any credit available.

I would tell them that they would be connected to a central call handling centre where they will be asked which service they require.

I would tell them that they must ask for the Fire Service. Once they are through to the operator they will be asked a series of important questions. I would tell them to listen carefully to the operator and answer all the questions carefully and accurately. It is important that they remain calm when making the call so that the operator can obtain all of the information.

I would tell them that the types of questions they will be asked are:

- *What the emergency is (e.g. fire, person stuck in a lift, road traffic collision, fire alarm sounding etc);*

- *Where it is (e.g. full address if known, name of road, prominent landmarks);*

- *How many people are involved, if any?*

- *Are there any injured people?*

- *Any specific problems/hazards that the Fire Service would need to be informed of.*

I would finally inform them that it is important to only use the 999 service when it is genuinely needed and that hoax calls should never be made."

SAMPLE QUESTION NUMBER 10

How do you think you would cope with working the Fire Service shift system?

Working unsociable hours is part and parcel of life in the Fire Service. You need to be 100% certain that you can cope with the irregular shift patterns and that your family supports you. Take a look at the following sample response.

Sample response
"I believe I would cope very well. I have taken into consideration the fact that I would be required to work unsociable hours and I am prepared for this. I have discussed it with my family and I have their full support. I have worked office based hours for many years now and I am actually looking forward to the change."

Finally, if you do already have experience of working unsociable and irregular hours, especially shift work, make sure you tell them this during the interview.

SAMPLE QUESTION NUMBER 11

Tell me about a time when you helped someone who was distressed or in need of support?

How to structure your response:

- What was the situation?

- Why did you provide the help? (Whether you were approached or you volunteered. It is better to say you volunteered!)

- What did you do to support the individual?

- What specifically did you do or say?

- What was the result?

Strong response

Make sure you provide a specific example of where you have helped someone who was in distress or who needed your support. Try to provide an example where the outcome was a positive one as a result of your actions. If the situation was one that involved potentially dangerous surroundings (such as a car accident), did you consider the safety aspect and did you carry out a risk assessment of the scene?

Weak response

Candidates who provide a weak response will be generic in their answering. The outcome of the situation will generally not be a positive one.

Sample response

"One evening I was sat at home watching television when I heard my next door neighbours smoke alarm sounding. This is not an unusual occurrence as she is always setting off the alarm whilst cooking. However, on this occasion, something

was different as the alarm did not normally sound so late at night. I got up out of my chair and went to see if she was OK. She is a vulnerable, elderly lady and I always look out for her whenever possible. When I arrived next door I peered through the window and noticed my neighbour sat asleep on the chair in the front room. Wisps of smoke were coming from the kitchen so I knew that she was in trouble. I immediately ran back into my house and dialled 999 calmly. I asked for the Fire Service and the Ambulance Service and explained that a person was stuck inside the house with a fire burning in the kitchen. I provided the call operator with as much information as possible including landmarks close to our road to make it easier for the Fire Service to find.

As soon as I got off the phone I immediately went round the back of my house to climb over the fence. Mrs Watson, my neighbour, usually leaves her back door unlocked until she goes to bed. I climbed over the fence and tried the door handle. Thankfully the door opened. I entered into the kitchen and turned off the gas hob which was burning dried up soup. I then ran to the front room, woke up Mrs Watson and carried her carefully through the front door, as this was the nearest exit. I then sat Mrs Watson down on the pavement outside and placed my coat around her. It wasn't long before the Fire Service arrived and took over from me. I gave them all of the details relating to the incident and informed them of my actions when in the kitchen."

SAMPLE QUESTION NUMBER 12

Tell me about a time when you had to follow clear instructions or rules in order to complete a task?

When working as a Fire Control Operator you will have to follow clear instructions at all times. This question will assess your ability to do just that during a work situation.

How to structure your response:

- What was the work you were doing?

- What were the rules or instructions that you had to follow?

- What did you do to complete the work as directed?

- What was the result?

- How did you feel about completing the task in this way?

Strong response
The Fire Service strives for excellence in everything it does. Therefore, it is crucial that you provide a response that demonstrates you too can deliver excellence and maintain high standards. Try to think of a situation, either at work or otherwise, where you have achieved this. Make your response specific in nature. If you have had to follow specific instructions, rules or procedures then this is a good thing to tell the panel.

Weak response
Weak responses are generic in nature and usually focus on a candidate's own views on how a task should be achieved, rather than in line with a company or organisation's policies and procedures. The candidate will display a lack of motivation in relation to following clear instructions or rules.

Sample response

"I am currently working as a sales assistant for a well-known retailer. I recently achieved a temporary promotion and part of that role includes carrying out preopening checks. I am required to get to work 60 minutes before opening time and carry out a comprehensive routine check. The work includes checking that all fire exits are unlocked, testing the fire alarm, assessing the current stock levels to make sure we have enough for the day's trade, turning on power and heating, checking the tills are stocked with cash, carrying out a risk assessment, briefing staff on safety hazards, briefing staff on the requirements for the day and liaising with the shopping centre manager. It is important that I follow the rules and instructions carefully because if I miss any of them off, the day's trading will not run smoothly and there could also be safety implications.

In order to make sure that I follow the instructions carefully I always make sure that I arrive at work with plenty of time to spare. This ensures that I leave plenty of time for any last minute hiccups. I also follow a self-made checklist, which I carry around with me on a clipboard. Once I have completed a task, I tick it off and write down any relevant notes that will help me to brief my staff. I always feel good about the manner in which I carry out my duties. I am an organised person and I take great pride in carrying out my duties both diligently and professionally."

SAMPLE QUESTION NUMBER 13

Can you provide an example of a situation when you have had to work under pressure?

The role of a Fire Control Operator will often require you to work under extreme pressure. Therefore, the recruitment staff will want to know that you have the ability to perform in such an environment. If you already have experience of working under pressure then you are far more likely to succeed and be capable of meeting the demands of the job. When responding to a question of this nature, try to provide an actual example of where you have achieved a task whilst being under pressure. Don't forget to follow the guidance at the beginning of this section, which related to responding effectively to interview questions using the STAR technique. Questions of this nature are sometimes included in the application form, so try to use a different example for the interview, if the question comes up.

Sample response

"Yes, I can. In my current job as car mechanic for a well-known company, I was presented with a difficult and pressurised situation. A member of the team had made a mistake and had fitted a number of wrong components to a car. The car in question was due to be picked up at 2pm and the customer had stated how important it was that his car was ready on time because he had an important meeting to attend. We only had two hours in which to resolve the issue and I volunteered to be the one who would carry out the work on the car. The problem was that we had 3 other customers in the workshop waiting for their cars too, so I was the only person who could be spared at that particular time. I worked solidly for the next 2 hours, making sure that I meticulously carried out each task in line with our operating procedures. Even though I didn't

finish the car until 2.10pm, I managed to achieve a very difficult task under pressurised conditions whilst following strict procedures and regulations. I understand that the role of a Fire Control Operator will require me to work under extreme pressure at times and I believe I have the experience to achieve this. I am very meticulous in my work and always ensure that I take personal responsibility to keep up-to-date with procedures and policies in my current job."

SAMPLE QUESTION NUMBER 14

What is Community Fire Safety?

If you are serious about joining the Fire Service then you should have some knowledge of Community Fire Safety.

Before preparing your answer to this question, read the Community Fire Safety (CFS) page on the website of the Fire Service you are applying to join, so that you can get a feel for what approach they are taking in relation to CFS. You may also wish to visit the Government's own Community Fire Safety site to get some more useful tips about this important subject. Whilst you may not get asked this type of questions at your FCOp interview, if you do, you will be far better prepared than the other candidates.

Now take a look at the following sample response.

Sample response

"Community Fire safety is one of the core elements of the role of the Fire Service.

It is about informing and educating the public with safety information that will help them to reduce the risk of fire in the home to nearly zero. It covers many different areas ranging from information relating to smoke alarms, home fire safety checks, electrical fire safety and cooking safety to name but a few. I am aware that the Fire Service is constantly looking for ways to reduce fire deaths and injuries in the home through its effective Community Fire Safety reduction strategies.

Community Fire Safety is also about working with other agencies including the Police and Social Services to establish ways of making the community safer together as opposed to working in isolation.

I visited your website and noticed that you have been working with Help the Aged to provide smoke alarms for the elderly, which is a good example of agencies working together to help save lives."

SAMPLE QUESTION NUMBER 15

Do you have any experience of working within the community?

Because the Fire Service is very much community based, the Fire Service want to know that you are able to work with people from all backgrounds.

People in the Fire Service have very good reputations for being caring, helpful and considerate people who will help out wherever possible. Whilst working as a Fire Control Operator you will not be out in the community working directly; however, you will be speaking to and communicating with people from the community. Therefore, it is important that you can provide examples of where you have already carried out some form of community work.

Community work can involve many different things ranging from Neighbourhood Watch to charity work or voluntary work.

Take a look at the following sample response.

Sample response

"I recently organised a charity boot fair at my local school. This was to try and raise money for a nearby hospital that wanted to buy some new medical equipment. I worked with a number of different people in the community to get the event off the ground.

I worked closely with the local school and advertised the boot fair in the local paper to try to generate some interest. I contacted local community groups such as Neighbourhood Watch to try to promote the event, which worked very well. The boot fair was attended by over 500 people and we managed to raise over £750 for the good cause. I wouldn't have been able to arrange the event without working closely with different people and groups from within the community.

how2become

The event was a great success and I plan to arrange another one next year."

SAMPLE QUESTION NUMBER 16

What do you understand by the term diversity?

You are almost guaranteed to be asked a question that relates to diversity and working with people from different cultures and backgrounds.

One of the Personal Qualities and Attributes of a Fire Control Operator is the ability to work with others. Over the last few years, Senior Fire Service stakeholders, in collaboration with the Government, have taken up the challenge to work towards a more diverse workforce. Therefore, an understanding of what diversity means, and how important it is to the Fire Service, is crucial if you are to become a competent Fire Control Operator. This particular question is designed to see if you understand what the term diversity means in relation to the Fire Service.

Take a look at the following sample response to this question.

Sample response
"The term diversity means different and varied.

For example, if the Fire Service has a diverse workforce, it means that the people in that workforce are from different backgrounds, cultures and genders. The community in which we live is extremely diverse. Therefore, it is important that the Fire Service represents the community in which it serves so that a high level of service can be maintained. This gives the public more confidence in the Fire Service.

There are also other added benefits of a diverse workforce. It enables the Fire Service to reach every part of the community and provide Fire Safety advice to everybody as opposed to just certain individual groups of people."

SAMPLE QUESTION NUMBER 17

What would be your reaction if someone you were working with was acting in an offensive manner?

This kind of behaviour is not tolerated and therefore you should be asking the person to stop acting in this offensive manner.

This type of behaviour includes any form of racial or sexual jokes and again, these are not tolerated within the UK Fire Service. The Fire Service has strict policies in relation to this kind of unacceptable behaviour and it will not be tolerated.

When responding to questions of this nature, you should say that you would take steps to stop the person from acting in this manner, either through intervention or reporting. However, only ever say these words if you actually mean it. Do not lie.

Take a look at the following sample response.

Sample response
What would be your reaction if someone you were working with was acting in an offensive manner?

"I would ask the person to stop. That would be my first action. This kind of behaviour is not acceptable. If I was to ignore it then I would be just as bad as the person who was carrying out the act.

I would then inform my Crew or Watch Manager about the behaviour so that he/she could decide if any further action needed to be taken."

SAMPLE QUESTION NUMBER 18

You are working as a Fire Control Operator, it is 4am and you receive a 999 call from an extremely distressed mother whose baby is trapped inside the house, which is ablaze. As you can imagine, she is extremely upset and is finding it hard to communicate with you on the phone. What would you do in this type of situation?

Sample response
"First of all, I would make sure I remained calm, in control and that I followed my training and operational procedures. The priority in this type of incident would be to get the fire crews and ambulance mobilised and en route as soon as possible. If there was a pre-alert system in place at control then I would put the bells down at the fire station which was located in the area that the call was made. This would give the crews time to get ready for dispatch.

I would communicate with the lady and make her aware that I would need the exact location of the incident so that the crews could be dispatched as soon as possible. If it was proving difficult to extract the information from her then I would remain calm but would try to assert how important the information was to us so that we could help her and her baby. I would also make other Fire Control Operators aware in the Control Centre of the incident so that they could listen out for further 999 calls from any other residents in the area. I would assume that in this type of incident multiple calls would be made at some point.

Once I had the exact address I would mobilise the crews stating the nature of the incident and that persons were trapped inside. I would then try to ascertain the location of the baby in the house. I would imagine that this type of information would be useful to fire crews en route to the

incident so that they could be prepared when they arrived. To summarise, the information I would ask the caller would be:

What the emergency, where it is (e.g. full address if known, name of road, prominent landmarks), how many people are involved, are there any injuries to personnel and are there any specific problems/hazards that we need to know about.

Finally, I would make sure that the caller did not go back into the house. If needed, and if I felt this was likely to be her next course of action, I would remain on the line talking to her to try and assure her and keep her as calm as possible. Once the crews arrive they would need to speak to her to gain further information and we would need her to be as calm as possible under the circumstances."

FINAL INTERVIEW TIPS AND ADVICE

- If you have prepared yourself fully leading up to the interview you will hopefully have the confidence to perform to the best of your ability on the day. As I mentioned at the beginning of this book, preparation is key to your success so take the time to follow the instructions and guidance provided within this section.

- Make sure you know the correct date, time and location of your interview and be there early, with plenty of time to spare.

- Take into account the possibility of heavy traffic, a breakdown and parking etc.

- It is a good idea to make sure you know exactly where you are going. I recommend you visit the interview location prior to the day so you are familiar with the location and how to get there.

- Ensure you have revisited your application form. They may ask you questions about its content so make sure you know what you submitted.

- Ensure you know about the role of the Fire Control Operator and information relating to the actual Fire and Rescue Service you are applying to join.

- Have some knowledge and understanding about Community Fire Safety before attending the interview. Whilst not essential, if you do get asked a question about what it is, you will be able to answer it correctly.

- Take a look at the Fire Service's website and find out what is current, such as Community Fire Safety campaigns, Integrated Risk Management and Incident Planning etc.

- It is always a good idea to arrange a visit to both a fire station and also the Fire Control Centre before your interview. Ask them questions about their role and their working day so that you are fully prepared for your interview.

- Be aware of the Race Equality Scheme for the Fire Service you are applying to join. You could be asked a question about equality and fairness during your interview. The Race Equality Scheme document should be available to download or read on the website of the Fire Service you are applying to join.

- Be aware of the Personal Qualities and Attributes that relate to the role of the Fire Control Operator. These are the areas that you will be assessed against. You must be able to provide specific examples of each key area.

- Make sure you dress smartly. Image is important in any interview and demonstrates that you are serious about the whole process. If you turn up in jeans and trainers the interviewer may view this as negative.

- Check if you are required to take anything with you such as references, certificates, driving licence or proof of your educational qualifications.

- Remember to smile during the interview and be positive.

- Think of two possible questions to ask at the end of the interview. Try not to be clever when asking questions but instead ask ones that are relevant such as "Where is the organisation planning to go with Community Fire Safety".

- When you enter the interview room make sure you are polite and say hello, good morning or good afternoon. Saying nothing at all will just come across as being rude.

- When you enter the interview room, don't sit down until invited to do so. Whilst this is not essential it does demonstrate good manners.

- Make sure you sit comfortably and don't slouch. A good posture will speak volumes about your confidence and determination to succeed.

- Think before you answer any questions. There is nothing wrong with pausing for a second to think about your answer. If you are unsure, ask them to repeat the question.

- Look interested when they are asking you questions and be positive in your answers.

- If you are unsure of an answer try not to 'waffle' or make something up. If you can't answer a question just be honest and move on.

- Speak up when answering any questions and make positive eye contact. This doesn't mean staring out the interviewer!

- Finally, don't over use your hands. Some hand movement or expression is good but too much can be distracting.

A FEW FINAL WORDS

You have now reached the end of the guide and no doubt you will be ready to apply to become a Fire Control Operator. The majority of candidates who pass the selection process have a number of common attributes. These are as follows:

1. They believe in themselves.

The first factor is self-belief. Regardless of what anyone tells you, you can become a Fire Control Operator. Just like any job of this nature, you have to be prepared to work hard in order to be successful. Make sure you have the self-belief to pass the selection process and fill your mind with positive thoughts.

2. They prepare fully.

The second factor is preparation. Those people who achieve in life prepare fully for every eventuality and that is what you must do when you apply to become a FCOp. Work very hard and especially concentrate on your weak areas.

3. They persevere.

Perseverance is a fantastic word. Everybody comes across obstacles or setbacks in their life, but it is what you do about those setbacks that is important. If you fail at something, then ask yourself 'why' you have failed. This will allow you to improve for next time and if you keep improving and trying, success will eventually follow. Apply this same method of thinking when you apply to become a Fire Control Operator.

4. They are self-motivated.

How much do you want this job? Do you want it, or do you really want it?

When you apply to join the Fire Service as a Fire Control Operator you should want it more than anything in the world. Your levels of self-motivation will shine through on your application and during your interview. For the weeks and months leading up to the selection process, be motivated as best you can and always keep your fitness levels up as this will serve to increase your levels of motivation.

Work hard, stay focused and be what you want...

Richard McMunn

P.S. You can get FREE access to sample psychometric tests online at the following website:

www.PsychometricTestsOnline.co.uk

how2become

Attend a 1-Day Fire Control Operator training course

www.FireControlOperator.co.uk